Windows Server® 2008 Enterprise Administrator (70-647)

Lab Manual

WILEY

EXECUTIVE EDITOR	John Kane
EDITORIAL PROGRAM ASSISTANT	Jennifer Lartz
DIRECTOR OF SALES	Mitchell Beaton
EXECUTIVE MARKETING MANAGER	Chris Ruel
CONTENT MANAGER	Micheline Frederick
PRODUCTION EDITOR	Amy Weintraub

Founded in 1807, John Wiley & Sons, Inc. has been a valued source of knowledge and understanding for more than 200 years, helping people around the world meet their needs and fulfill their aspirations. Our company is built on a foundation of principles that include responsibility to the communities we serve and where we live and work. In 2008, we launched a Corporate Citizenship Initiative, a global effort to address the environmental, social, economic, and ethical challenges we face in our business. Among the issues we are addressing are carbon impact, paper specifications and procurement, ethical conduct within our business and among our vendors, and community and charitable support. For more information, please visit our website: www.wiley.com/go/citizenship.

To order books or for customer service, please call 1-800-CALL WILEY (225-5945).

ISBN 978-0-470-22517-2

Printed in the United States of America

10 9 8 7 6 5 4 3 2

BRIEF CONTENTS

CONTENTS

LAB 1
CONFIGURING A DOMAIN CONTROLLER

This lab contains the following exercises and activities:

Exercise 1.1   Configuring Time Zone Settings

Exercise 1.2   Configuring the TCP/IP Client

Exercise 1.3   Configuring the Server Name

Exercise 1.4   Installing the Active Directory Domain Services Role

Exercise 1.5   Promoting the Server to a Domain Controller

BEFORE YOU BEGIN

The lab environment consists of student servers connected to a local area network, along with a classroom server that functions as the domain controller for a domain called contoso.com. Each student will have his or her own server, on which the student will create a domain controller for a new forest. Most of the exercises in this manual will require each student to work on his or her own domain controller in a separate Active Directory Domain Services domain.

NOTE	In the classroom lab environment, the instructor will assign each server a number that the student will use to form the server's IP address, computer name, and domain name. This will keep each server in its own separate environment and prevent server interaction until it is specifically needed.

In addition to the computers, you will also require the software listed in Table 1-1 to complete Lab 1.

Table 1-1
Software required for Lab 1

Software	Location
Lab 1 student worksheet	Lab01_worksheet.rtf (provided by instructor)

Working with Lab Worksheets

Each lab in this manual requires that you answer questions, shoot screen shots, and perform other activities that you will document in a worksheet named for the lab, such as Lab01_worksheet.rtf. Your instructor will provide you with access to the worksheets. It is recommended that you use a USB flash drive to store your worksheets, so you can submit them to your instructor for review. As you perform the exercises in each lab, open the appropriate worksheet file using WordPad, fill in the required information, and save the file to your flash drive.

SCENARIO

You are an enterprise administrator who is preparing a lab environment in which you will test various Windows Server 2008 R2 technologies and procedures, enabling you to devise policies that you will deploy throughout your organization's enterprise network.

After completing this lab, you will be able to:

■ Prepare a lab server to function as an Active Directory Domain Services domain controller

Estimated lab time: 50 minutes

Exercise 1.1	Configuring Time Zone Settings
Overview	Configure the time zone settings of a newly installed computer running Windows Server 2008 R2.
Completion time	10 minutes

1. Turn on your Windows Server 2008 R2 server.

2. Press Ctrl+Alt+Del. The Windows logon page appears.

3. In the Password text box, type **Pa$$w0rd**. Then click the right arrow button to log on. The Initial Configuration Tasks window appears, as shown in Figure 1-1.

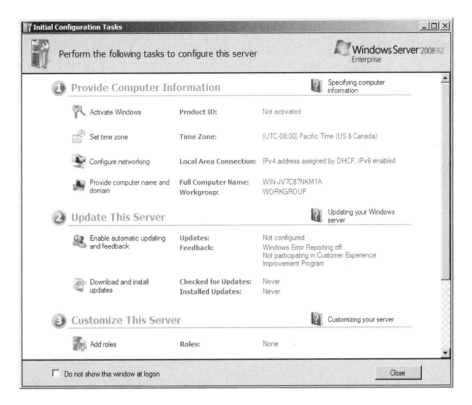

Figure 1-1
The Initial Configuration Tasks window

4. Click *Set time zone*. The Date and Time dialog box appears.

5. Click *Change time zone*. The Time Zone Settings dialog box appears.

6. In the Time zone drop-down list, select the appropriate time zone for your location and click *OK*.

7. Check the currently displayed time, and if necessary, click *Change date and time* to open the Date and Time Settings dialog box, in which you can change it.

8. Click *OK* to close the Date and Time dialog box.

9. Open your Lab01_worksheet file in WordPad and answer the following questions.

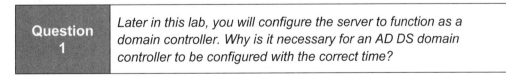

Question 1	*Later in this lab, you will configure the server to function as a domain controller. Why is it necessary for an AD DS domain controller to be configured with the correct time?*

10. Close the worksheet file, saving your work to your USB flash drive.

11. Leave the server logged on for the next exercise.

Exercise 1.2	Configuring the TCP/IP Client
Overview	Configure the network interface adapter on your server with an appropriate IP address.
Completion time	10 minutes

1.   In the Initial Configuration Tasks window, click *Configure networking*. The Network Connections window appears.

2.   Right-click the *Local Area Connection* icon and, from the context menu, select *Properties*. The Local Area Connection Properties sheet appears.

3.   Select Internet Protocol Version 4 (TCP/IPv4) and click *Properties*. The Internet Protocol Version 4 (TCP/IPv4) Properties sheet appears, as shown in Figure 1-2.

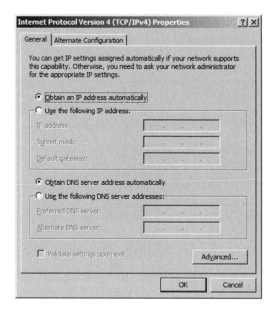

Figure 1-2
The Internet Protocol Version 4 (TCP/IPv4)
Properties sheet

4.   Select the *Use the following IP address* option.

5.   In the IP address text box, type **10.0.xx.1**, where *xx* is the number your instructor assigned to your server.

6.   In the Subnet mask text box, type **255.255.255.0**.

7.   In the Preferred DNS server text box, type **127.0.0.1**.

8.   Click *OK* to close the Internet Protocol Version 4 (TCP/IPv4) Properties sheet.

9.   Select Internet Protocol Version 6 (TCP/IPv6) and click *Properties*. The Internet Protocol Version 6 (TCP/IPv6) Properties sheet appears.

10. Select the *Use the following IP address* option.

11. In the IPv6 address text box, type **fec0:0:0:fffe::1**. The value **64** appears in the Subnet prefix length text box and the value **::1** appears in the Preferred DNS server text box.

12. Click *OK* to close the Internet Protocol Version 6 (TCP/IPv6) Properties sheet.

13. Click *OK* to close the Local Area Connection Properties sheet.

14. Close the Network Connections window.

15. Leave the server logged on for the next exercise.

Exercise 1.3	Configuring the Server Name
Overview	Configure your server with a unique name.
Completion time	10 minutes

1. In the Initial Configuration Tasks window, click *Provide computer name and domain*. The System Properties sheet appears.

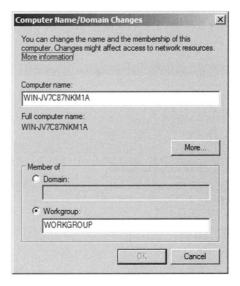

Figure 1-3
The Computer Name/Domain Changes
dialog box

2. Click *Change*. The Computer Name/Domain Changes dialog box appears, as shown in Figure 1-3.

3. In the Computer name text box, type **SVRxx**, where *xx* is the number your instructor assigned to your server.

4.   Click *OK*. A Computer Name/Domain Changes message box appears, prompting you to restart the computer.

5.   Click *OK*. The message box closes.

6.   Click *OK* to close the System Properties sheet. A Microsoft Windows message box appears, prompting you again to restart the computer.

7.   Click *Restart Now*. The computer restarts.

Exercise 1.4	Installing the Active Directory Domain Services Role
Overview	Configure the network interface adapter on your server with an appropriate IP address.
Completion time	5 minutes

1.   Press Ctrl+Alt+Del. The Windows logon page appears.

2.   In the Password text box, type **Pa$$w0rd**. Then click the right arrow button to log on. The Initial Configuration Tasks window appears.

3.   Click *Add roles*. The Add Roles Wizard appears.

4.   Click *Next* to bypass the *Before You Begin* page. The *Select Server Roles* page appears, as shown in Figure 1-4.

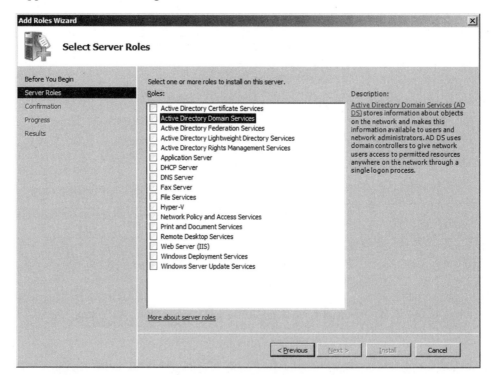

Figure 1-4
The *Select Server Roles* page of the Add Roles Wizard

5. Select the Active Directory Domain Services check box. The Add features required for Active Directory Domain Services? dialog box appears.

6. Click *Add Required Features*. Then, on the *Select Server Roles* page, click *Next*. The *Active Directory Domain Services* page appears.

7. Click *Next*. The *Confirm Installation Selections* page appears.

8. Click *Install*. The wizard installs the role and the *Installation Results* page appears.

9. Click *Close*. The wizard closes.

10. Leave the server logged on for the next exercise.

Exercise 1.5	Promoting the Server to a Domain Controller
Overview	Configure the network interface adapter on your server with an appropriate IP address.
Completion time	15 minutes

1. Click *Start*. Then, in the Search programs and files text box, type **dcpromo** and press *Enter*. The Active Directory Domain Services Installation Wizard appears.

2. Click *Next* to bypass the *Welcome* page. The *Operating System Compatibility* page appears.

3. Click *Next*. The *Choose a Deployment Configuration* page appears.

4. Select the Create a new domain in a new forest option and click *Next*. The *Name the Forest Root Domain* page appears.

5. In the FQDN of the forest root domain text box, type **contoso*xx*.com**, where *xx* is the number your instructor assigned to your server, and then click *Next*. The *Set Forest Functional Level* page appears.

6. In the Forest functional level drop-down list, select Windows Server 2008 R2 and click *Next*. The *Additional Domain Controller options* page appears.

7. Click *Next* to accept the default settings. An Active Directory Domain Services Installation Wizard message box appears, warning of inability to create a delegation for the DNS server.

8. Click *Yes*. The *Location or Database, Log Files, and SYSVOL* page appears.

9. Click *Next* to accept the default settings. The *Directory Services Restore Mode Administrator Password* page appears.

10. In the Password and Confirm password text boxes, type **Pa$$w0rd** and click *Next*. The *Summary* page appears.

11. Click *Next*. The wizard installs Active Directory Domain Services, and the *Completing the Active Directory Domain Services Installation Wizard* page appears.

12. Click *Finish*. An Active Directory Domain Services Installation Wizard message box appears, prompting you to restart the computer.

13. Click *Restart Now*. The computer restarts.

14. Press Ctrl+Alt+Del. The Windows logon page appears.

15. In the Password text box, type **Pa$$w0rd**. Then click the right arrow button to log on. The Initial Configuration Tasks window appears.

16. Take a screen shot of the Initial Configuration Tasks window, showing the changes you made in this lab, by pressing Alt+Prt Scr, and then paste it into your Lab01_worksheet file in the page provided by pressing Ctrl+V.

17. Log off of the server.

LAB 2
WORKING WITH DHCP AND DNS

This lab contains the following exercises and activities:

BEFORE YOU BEGIN

The lab environment consists of student servers connected to a local area network, along with a classroom server that functions as the domain controller for a domain called contoso.com. Each student has his or her own server, which functions as a domain controller for a separate forest. Most of the exercises in this manual will require each student to work on his or her own domain controller in a separate Active Directory Domain Services domain.

> **NOTE**
> *In the classroom lab environment, the instructor has assigned each server a number that the student will use to form the server's IP address, computer name, and domain name, as specified in Lab 1. This will keep each server in its own separate environment and prevent server interaction until it is specifically needed. You must complete Lab 1 before you proceed with the exercises in this lab.*

In addition to the computers, you will also require the software listed in Table 2-1 to complete Lab 2.

Table 2-1
Software required for Lab 2

Software	Location
Lab 2 student worksheet	Lab02_worksheet.rtf (provided by instructor)

Working with Lab Worksheets

Each lab in this manual requires that you answer questions, shoot screen shots, and perform other activities that you will document in a worksheet named for the lab, such as Lab02_worksheet.rtf. Your instructor will provide you with access to the worksheets. It is recommended that you use a USB flash drive to store your worksheets, so you can submit them to your instructor for review. As you perform the exercises in each lab, open the appropriate worksheet file using WordPad, fill in the required information, and save the file to your flash drive.

SCENARIO

You are an enterprise administrator working in a lab environment in which you are testing designs for the Windows Server 2008 R2 infrastructure services that your company will need for a new division it is deploying in the near future.

After completing this lab, you will be able to:

- Install and configure a DHCP server

- Design a DNS namespace

- Configure a DNS server

Estimated lab time: 90 minutes

Exercise 2.1	Installing the DHCP Role
Overview	DHCP enables computers on the lab network to obtain their own IP addresses and other critical TCP/IP settings. To deploy a DHCP server, you must first install the DHCP role using Server Manager.
Completion time	15 minutes

1. Log on to your server using the **Administrator** account and the password **Pa$$w0rd**. The Initial Configuration Tasks window appears.

2. Click *Start*, point to Administrative Tools, and click *Server Manager*. The Server Manager console appears.

3. Select the Roles node and click *Add Roles*. The Add Roles Wizard appears, displaying the *Before You Begin* page.

4. Click *Next* to continue. The *Select Server Roles* page appears.

5. Select the DHCP Server check box and click *Next*. The *DHCP Server* page appears.

6. Click *Next*. The *Select Network Connection Bindings* page appears, as shown in Figure 2-1.

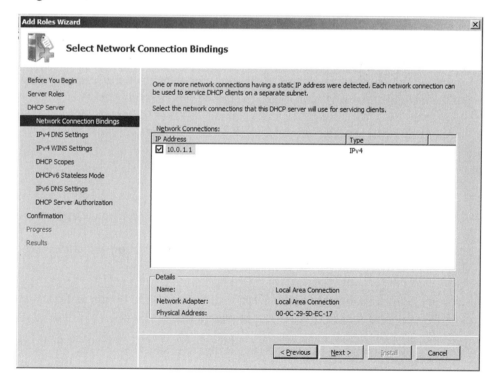

Figure 2-1
The *Select Network Connection Bindings* page of the Add Roles Wizard

Question 1	*Where did the wizard obtain the IP address that appears on the Select Network Connection Bindings page?*

7. Click *Next* to accept the default settings. The *Specify IPv4 DNS Server Settings* page appears.

Question 2	*Where did the wizard obtain the loopback address that appears in the Preferred DNS Server IPv4 Address text box?*

Question 3	*What would happen if you left the loopback address in the Preferred DNS Server IPv4 Address text box?*

8. In the Preferred DNS Server IPv4 Address text box, type the IP address you assigned to your server in Lab 1-2, using the form **10.0.xx.1**, where *xx* is the number your instructor assigned to your server.

9. Click the *Validate* button.

Question 4	*What happens?*

10. Take a screen shot of the Add Roles Wizard, showing the *Specify IPv4 DNS Server Settings* page, by pressing Ctrl+Prt Scr, and then paste the resulting image into the lab02_worksheet file in the page provided by pressing Ctrl+V.

11. Click *Next* to continue. The *Specify IPv4 WINS Server Settings* page appears.

12. Click *Next* to accept the default settings. The *Add or Edit DHCP Scopes* page appears.

13. Click *Next* to continue. The *Configure DHCPv6 Stateless Mode* page appears.

14. Select the Disable DHCPv6 stateless mode for the server option and click *Next*. The *Authorize DHCP Server* page appears.

15. Select the Skip authorization of this DHCP server in AD DS option and click *Next*. The *Confirm Installation Selections* page appears.

16. Click *Install*. The wizard installs the DHCP Server role.

17. Click *Close*. The wizard closes.

18. Close the Server Manager console.

19. Leave the computer logged on for the next exercise.

Exercise 2.2	Creating a DHCPv4 Scope
Overview	A scope is a range of IP addresses that a DHCP server uses to supply clients on a particular subnet with IP addresses. Create a scope for IPv4 addresses on your DHCP server.
Completion time	15 minutes

1. Click *Start*, point to Administrative Tools, and click *DHCP*. The DHCP console appears, as shown in Figure 2-2.

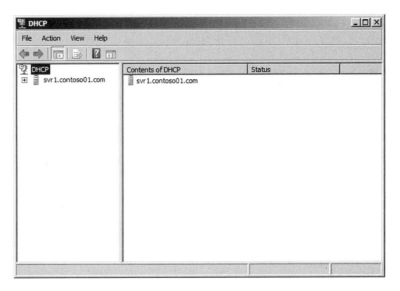

Figure 2-2
The DHCP console

2. Expand the *svrxx.contoso.com* node.

3. Right-click the IPv4 node and, from the context menu, select *New Scope*. The New Scope wizard appears.

4. Click *Next* to bypass the *Welcome* page. The *Scope Name* page appears.

5. In the *Name* text box, type **10.0.xx.0,** where *xx* is the number your instructor assigned to your server and click *Next*. The *IP Address Range* page appears.

6. In the Start IP address text box, type **10.1.xx.1**, where *xx* is the number your instructor assigned to your server.

7. In the End IP address text box, key **10.1.xx.100,** where *xx* is the number your instructor assigned to your server.

Question 5	*Notice that the wizard automatically adds a value to the Subnet mask text box. Where did this value come from?*

8. In the Subnet mask text box, key **255.255.255.0**. Then click *Next*. The *Add Exclusions and Delay* page appears.

9. In the Start IP address text box, key **10.1.xx.1**.

10. In the End IP address text box, type **10.1.xx.24**.

11. Click *Add*. The address appears in the Excluded address range list.

12. Click *Next*. The *Lease Duration* page appears.

13. Click *Next* to accept the default value. The *Configure DHCP Options* page appears.

14. Click *Next* to accept the Yes, I want to configure these options now option. The *Router (Default Gateway)* page appears.

15. In the IP address text box, key **10.0.xx.1** and then click *Add*.

16. Click *Next* to continue. The *Domain Name and DNS Servers* page appears.

17. In the Parent domain text box, the name of the forest root domain you specified in Exercise 1.4 should appear.

18. In the Server name text box, type **SVRxx**, where *xx* is the number your server assigned to your server click *Resolve*. Your computer's IP address appears in the adjacent text box.

19. Click *Add*.

20. In the IP address list, select 127.0.0.1 and click *Remove*.

21. Click *Next*. The *WINS Servers* page appears.

22. Click *Next* to bypass the page. The *Activate Scope* page appears.

23. Click *Next* to accept the default Yes, I want to activate this scope now option. The *Completing the New Scope Wizard* page appears.

24. Click *Finish*. The scope is added to the console.

25. Expand the IPv4 node and the new scope, and then select the Address Pool folder.

26. Take a screen shot of the DHCP console, showing the contents of the Address Pool folder, by pressing Ctrl+Prt Scr, and then paste the resulting image into the lab02_worksheet file in the page provided by pressing Ctrl+V.

27. Leave the DHCP console open for the next exercise.

Exercise 2.3	Creating a DHCPv6 Scope
Overview	Create a DHCP scope to allocate IPv6 addresses to the computers on your network.
Completion time	15 minutes

1. In the DHCP console, right-click the IPv6 node and, from the context menu, select *New Scope*. The New Scope Wizard for IPv6 addresses appears.

2. Click *Next* to bypass the *Welcome* page. The *Scope Name* page appears.

3. In the Name text box, type **IPv6 *xx***, where *xx* is the number your instructor assigned to your server. Then click *Next*. The *Scope Prefix* page appears, as shown in Figure 2-3.

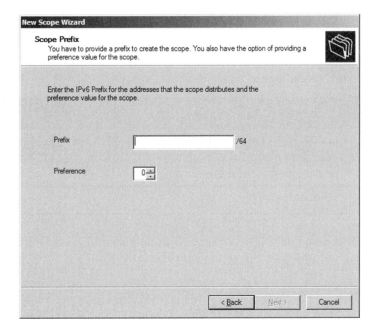

Figure 2-3
The *Scope Prefix* page in the New Scope Wizard

4. In the Prefix text box, type **fec0::fffe** and click *Next*. The *Add Exclusions* page appears.

5. In the Start IPv6 address text box, type **0:0:0:1**.

6. In the End IPv6 address text box, type **0:0:0:ff** and click *Add*. The range appears in the Excluded address range list.

7. Click *Next*. The *Scope Lease* page appears.

8. Click *Next*. The *Completing the New Scope Wizard* page appears.

9. Click *Finish*. The wizard creates the scope.

10. Expand the IPv6 xx scope you just created.

11. Right-click the Scope Options node and, from the context menu, select Configure Options. The Scope Options dialog box appears.

12. Select the check box for the DNS Recursive Name Server IPv6 Address List option.

13. In the New IPv6 address list, type **fec0:0:0:fffe::1** and click *Add*. The address appears in the Current IPv6 address list.

Question 6	Where did the **fec0:0:0:fffe::1** address come from that you supplied for the DNS Recursive Name Server IPv6 Address List option?

14. Take a screen shot of the Scope Options dialog box, showing the option you just configured, by pressing Ctrl+Prt Scr, and then paste the resulting image into the lab02_worksheet file in the page provided by pressing Ctrl+V.

15. Click *OK* to close the Scope Options dialog box.

16. Close the DHCP console.

17. Leave the workstation logged on for the next exercise.

Exercise 2.4	Designing a DNS Namespace
Overview	The new division will have its own DNS namespace, and your first task is to design that namespace by specifying appropriate domain and host names for the computers in the division.
Completion time	15 minutes

1. Design a DNS namespace for your organization that conforms to the following guidelines:

- The root domain name for the organization is contosoxx.com, where xx is the number your instructor has assigned to your server. All of the additional domains you create must be subordinate to this domain.

- The internal network must be in a different domain from the external network.

- The organization has three internal divisions: Sales, Human Resources, and Production. Each division must be represented by a separate subdomain in the namespace.

- Each division has departmental servers performing various roles and as many as 200 workstations, only some of which are shown in the diagram. Your host names should identify the function of each computer.

- Three servers on an external perimeter network host the company's Internet services: Web, FTP, and email. These servers must be in the domain contosoxx.com.

2. On the worksheet provided in Figure 2-4, on the following page, write the domain names and the fully qualified domain names you have selected for the computers in the appropriate spaces.

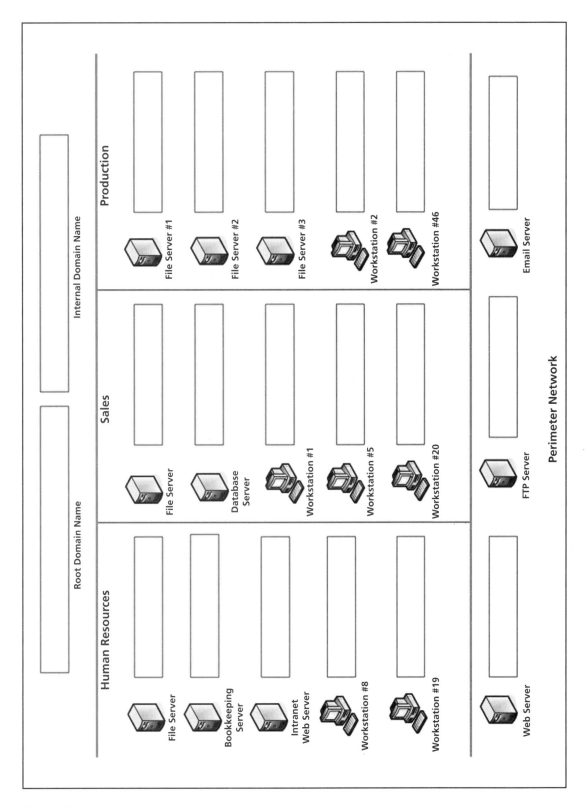

Figure 2-4
DNS namespace design worksheet

Exercise 2.5	Creating a DNS Zone
Overview	The zone is the administrative division that DNS servers use to separate domains. The first step in implementing the DNS namspace you designed is to create a zone representing your root domain.
Completion time	10 minutes

1. Click *Start*, and then click *Administrative Tools > DNS*. The DNS Manager console appears.

2. Expand the SVR*xx* node and select the Forward Lookup Zones folder, as shown in Figure 2-5.

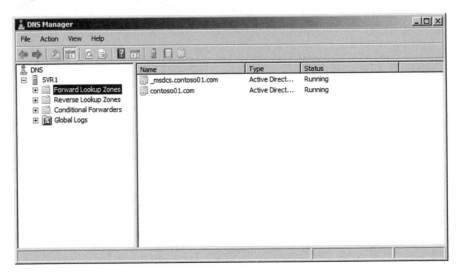

Figure 2-5
The DNS Manager console

Question 7	*Why is a zone for the root domain of your DNS namespace already present in the Forward Lookup Zones folder?*

3. Right-click the *Forward Lookup Zones* folder and, from the context menu, select *New Zone*. The New Zone Wizard appears.

4. Click *Next* to bypass the *Welcome* page. The *Zone Type* page appears.

5. Leave the Primary Zone option and the Store the zone in Active Directory check box selected and click *Next*. The *Active Directory Zone Replication Scope* page appears.

6. Click *Next* to accept the default setting. The *Zone Name* page appears.

7. In the Zone Name text box, type the internal domain name from the diagram you created in Exercise 2-4 and click *Next*. The *Dynamic Update* page appears.

8. Select the Allow both nonsecure and secure dynamic updates option and click *Next*. The *Completing the New Zone Wizard* page appears.

9. Click *Finish*. The new zone appears in the Forward Lookup Zones folder in the console.

Question 8	What resource records appear in the new zone you created by default?

10. Leave the DNS Manager console open for the next exercise.

Exercise 2.6	Creating DNS Domains
Overview	A single zone on a DNS server can encompass multiple domains, as long as the domains are contiguous. Create the departmental domains you specified in your namespace design.
Completion time	5 minutes

1. In the DNS Manager console, right-click the zone you created using the internal domain name from your namespace in Exercise 2-5 and, from the context menu, select *New Domain*. The New DNS Domain dialog box appears, as shown in Figure 2-6.

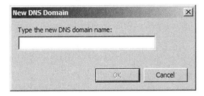

Figure 2-6
The New DNS Domain dialog box

2. In the Type the new DNS domain name text box, type the name of the Human Resources domain you specified in your namespace design and click *OK*.

NOTE	*When you create a domain within a zone, you specify the name for the new domain relative to the zone name. For example, to create the hr.int.contoso.com domain in the int.contoso.com zone, you would specify only the hr name in the New DNS Domain dialog box.*

3. Repeat steps 1 to 2 to create the domains for the Sales and Production departments from your namespace design.

Question 9	What resource records appear in the new domains you created by default?

4. Leave the DNS Manager console open for the next exercise.

Exercise 2.7	Creating DNS Resource Records
Overview	Now that you have created the zones and domains for your namespace, you can begin to populate them with the resource records that the DNS server uses to resolve host names into IP addresses.
Completion time	15 minutes

1. In the DNS Manager console, right-click your root domain zone and, from the context menu, select *New Host* (A or AAA). The New Host dialog box appears, as shown in Figure 2-7.

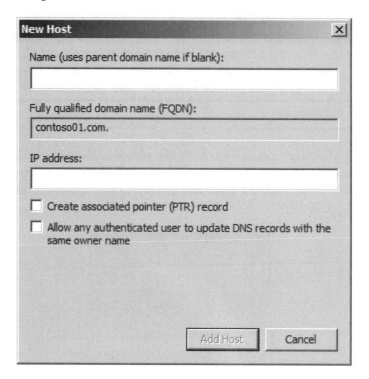

Figure 2-7
The New Host dialog box

2. In the Name text box, type the host name of the Internet web server you specified in your namespace design.

3. In the IP Address text box, key **10.1.xx.11,** where *xx* is the number your instructor assigned to your server.

4. Click *Add Host*. A DNS message box appears, stating that the resource record was created.

Question 10	What must you do before you can select the Create associated pointer (PTR) record check box in the New Host dialog box?

5.   Click *OK*. A new, blank Add Host dialog box appears.

6.   Repeat steps 2 to 4 to create Host records for the Internet FTP and Internet email servers in your namespace design, using the IP addresses 10.1.*xx*.12 and 10.1.*xx*.13, respectively.

7.   In the three domains you created in Exercise 2.6, create Host resource records for all of the remaining computers in your namespace design, using the names you specified in your diagram and different IP addresses in the 10.1.*xx*.2 to 10.1.*xx*.24 range.

> **NOTE**
>
> *For the purposes of this exercise, the IP addresses you use when creating your resource records do not matter. In an actual DNS deployment, you must either specify an appropriate IP address for each host, based on the subnet to which the computer is connected, or rely on DHCP to create the resource records for the computers.*

8.   Click *Done* to close the Add Host dialog box.

9.   Take a screen shot of the DNS Manager console, showing the resource records you created in the Human Resources domain, by pressing Ctrl+Prt Scr, and then paste the resulting image into the Lab02_worksheet file in the page provided by pressing Ctrl+V.

10.   Close the DNS Manager console.

LAB 3
CREATING FOREST AND DOMAIN DESIGNS

This lab contains the following exercises and activities:

Exercise 3.1   Drawing a Network Diagram

Exercise 3.2   Designing a Forest Strategy

Exercise 3.3   Designing a Domain Strategy

Exercise 3.4   Diagramming Forests and Domains

BEFORE YOU BEGIN

This lab consists of exercises that require only pencil and paper, or suitable drawing and word-processing software.

SCENARIO

Contoso Ltd. is an aeronautical engineering firm that conceives, designs, and builds electronic navigation and warfare components for manufacturers of military and commercial airplanes around the world. The company has offices and plants in various cities around the United States, and has recently acquired a firm called Trey Research, which specializes in the development of high-performance targeting scanners.

Contoso is nearly ready to sign a contract with a major aircraft manufacturer to supply components for a new U.S. military fighter plane that is about to go into production. The company has already invested an enormous amount of time and money, including the Trey Research purchase, into the project. However, they have recently been informed that, in order to supply products for a government contract, their data networks must meet certain reliability and security requirements. You have been assigned the task of evaluating those requirements and designing an Active Directory Domain Services solution that meets those requirements.

Facilities

The corporate headquarters and primary manufacturing facility for Contoso is located in Houston, Texas. The Houston facility has approximately 2,000 servers and workstations, a large centralized IT staff, and a perimeter network containing all of the servers that provides web, email, and other Internet services for the entire company.

Contoso also has two other main locations, in San Francisco, California, and New York, New York. The San Francisco site houses a research and development facility that currently has 750 workstations and servers, and which the company will be doubling in size to accommodate the new contract. They have a small IT staff to maintain their local servers, but they obtain most of their corporate resources, such as company databases and email, from the Houston office.

The sales and marketing office in New York has 75 users and some high-powered graphics workstations, but their only local servers are used for file storage. There are some users at the site with networking experience, but no dedicated IT staff.

The Houston and San Francisco offices are connected by a dedicated T-3 line that provides 44.7 megabits per second (Mbps) of bandwidth. The New York office is connected to Houston by a dedicated T-1 line running at 1.5 Mbps. There is no direct connection between the New York and San Francisco offices. Each of the three offices also has a 1.5 Mbps connection to the Internet.

Trey Research, based in Seattle, Washington, is a design firm that has only recently been acquired by Contoso, Ltd. They are responsible for a good deal of the most advanced technology in the new fighter aircraft. Their facility supports 500 users, 400 of which are the technical design staff. The other 100 are support staff, most of which will be transferred to the other Contoso offices or made redundant. The existing IT staff, however, will remain.

Contoso's plan is for the Trey designers and the San Francisco R&D staff to work closely together, creating new technology for current and future government projects. They have just recently installed a T-3 connection between the Seattle and San Francisco sites and a T-1 connecting Seattle and Houston.

Contoso's plan is to augment the Trey designer staff with selected personnel from the San Francisco R&D office and use the fabrication facilities in San Francisco to develop prototypes. This new unit will be known as Trey Contoso. The two offices will therefore work closely together, creating new technology for current and future government projects. However, part of the San Francisco staff will still be devoted to ongoing Contoso projects.

Requirements

Contoso's current AD DS infrastructure was designed nearly ten years ago, when Active Directory was a relatively new technology. The IT director at the time created a single forest with a single domain for the entire corporation, and ever since then, the IT staff has been making do with that arrangement. As the company has grown, the AD infrastructure has become increasingly inefficient, so the management has decided that this is the appropriate time for a complete Active Directory redesign effort.

The new contract, and specifically the work being done by the Trey Contoso division, falls under government regulations for classified technology that impose highly specific requirements on the AD DS infrastructure. The Trey Contoso division must be administratively isolated from the rest of the company, and within that division, forest-level services must be administered by a different IT operations team than the domain-level services.

The research and development department at Trey Contoso also has special security requirements that are different from those in the rest of the division. The Trey Contoso division must not host any services on the Internet. Government standards also require 16-character complex passwords for the R&D accounts, assigned weekly by the network administrators, not chosen by the users themselves. The rest of the Trey Contoso division will use self-assigned eight-character passwords. Because there are still some domain controllers that have not been upgraded to Windows Server 2008, fine-grained password policies are not yet supported.

In the Contoso division, based in Houston, the issue is not requirements imposed by outside bodies, but performance goals dictated by the management. When the IT staff first installed Active Directory, the company's Internet services consisted of one single computer that functioned as both web server and FTP server. Today, the perimeter network contains dozens of servers, functioning as a web farm that hosts sites and applications for employees, existing customers, and potential clients. Because the perimeter network is currently not part of the AD DS infrastructure, keeping all the servers properly configured and updated has become an extremely time-consuming job. As part of this project, the management wants the perimeter network to be added to the AD DS infrastructure, while still being isolated from the internal network resources that need protection from the Internet.

Replication traffic between domain controllers has become an increasingly serious problem in recent years as the network has grown. The management expects the AD DS redesign to minimize the bandwidth consumed by replication on the links between the sites. The current AD DS design has domain controllers located only in the Houston and San Francisco sites, with the T-3 connection largely consumed by replication traffic. The New York office uses its T-1 connection to access domain controllers at the other sites, which provides lackluster performance. Management expects the new design to include domain controllers at all four sites in order to provide improved performance, and a newly designed domain and site strategy in order to minimize bandwidth utilization.

After completing this lab, you will be able to:

■ Draw a network diagram

■ Create a forest design strategy

■ Create a domain design strategy

Estimated lab time: 80 minutes

Exercise 3.1	Drawing a Network Diagram
Overview	The first step in redesigning the AD DS infrastructure is to diagram the physical network architecture.
Completion time	20 minutes

1. To complete this exercise, draw a diagram representing the physical architecture of the Contoso network as it currently exists. The diagram should include all of the company sites (including new acquisitions), the number of computers at each site, the connections between the sites, and the bandwith of each connection. You can use either pencil and paper or a software product with suitable drawing tools to create your diagram.

Exercise 3.2	Designing a Forest Strategy
Overview	Create a forest strategy for Contoso, Ltd. that meets the requirements specified in the scenario.
Completion time	20 minutes

1. Using the requirements stated in the scenario, create an AD DS forest strategy for the Contoso, Ltd. network. Your strategy should specify how many forests are needed and provide the following information for each forest:

    • Forest name

    • Why a separate forest is required

    • Which forest model the forest should use

    • What resources should be included in the forest

Exercise 3.3	Designing a Domain Strategy
Overview	Create a domain strategy for Contoso, Ltd. that meets the requirements specified in the scenario.
Completion time	20 minutes

1. Using the requirements stated in the scenario, create an domain strategy for each of the forests you specified in Exercise 3.2. Your strategy should specify how many domains will be needed in each forest and provide the following information for each domain:

    -   Domain name

    -   Why a separate domain is required

    -   What resources should be included in the domain

    -   Where the domain controllers for the domain should be located

    -   Whether the forest should have a dedicated root domain

Exercise 3.4	Diagramming Forests and Domains
Overview	Create a diagram of the forest and domain strategies you designed in Exercises 3.2 and 3.3.
Completion time	20 minutes

1. Create a diagram of the forests and domains in your design, indicating the name of each forest and the domains each forest contains.

LAB 4
CONFIGURING SITES AND REPLICATION

This lab contains the following exercises and activities:

BEFORE YOU BEGIN

The lab environment consists of student servers connected to a local area network, along with a classroom server that functions as the domain controller for a domain called contoso.com. Each student has his or her own server, which functions as a domain controller for a separate forest. Most of the exercises in this manual will require each student to work on his or her own domain controller in a separate Active Directory Domain Services domain.

> **NOTE**
>
> *In the classroom lab environment, the instructor has assigned each server a number that the student will use to form the server's IP address, computer name, and domain name, as specified in Lab 1. This will keep each server in its own separate environment and prevent server interaction until it is specifically needed. You must complete Lab 1 before you proceed with the exercises in this lab.*

In addition to the computers, you will also require the software listed in Table 4-1 to complete Lab 4.

Table 4-1
Software required for Lab 4

Software	Location
Lab 4 student worksheet	Lab04_worksheet.rtf (provided by instructor)

Working with Lab Worksheets

Each lab in this manual requires that you answer questions, shoot screen shots, and perform other activities that you will document in a worksheet named for the lab, such as Lab04_worksheet.rtf. Your instructor will provide you with access to the worksheets. It is recommended that you use a USB flash drive to store your worksheets, so you can submit them to your instructor for review. As you perform the exercises in each lab, open the appropriate worksheet file using WordPad, fill in the required information, and save the file to your flash drive.

SCENARIO

You are an enterprise administrator working in a lab environment where you are testing designs for the Windows Server 2008 R2 infrastructure services that your company will need for a new division it is deploying in the near future. In your current lab scenario, an organization with branch offices of various sizes all over the United States is installing an Active Directory Domain Services network using a single forest and a single domain. Hoowever, because the various offices are connected using links running at different speeds, it will be necessary for you to create multiple sites, to regulate the replication traffic.

After completing this lab, you will be able to:

- Create Active Directory Domain Services site objects

- Create subnet objects

- Create site objects

- Create site link objects

- Calculate site link costs

Estimated lab time: 90 minutes

Exercise 4.1	Creating Site Objects
Overview	Create site objects in your domain representing the various locations where your company has branch offices.
Completion time	15 minutes

1. Log on to your server using the **Administrator** account and the password **Pa$$w0rd**. The Initial Configuration Tasks window appears.

2. Click *Start*. Then click *Administrative Tools > Active Directory Sites and Services*. The Active Directory Sites and Services console appears.

3. Expand the Sites folder, as shown in Figure 4-1.

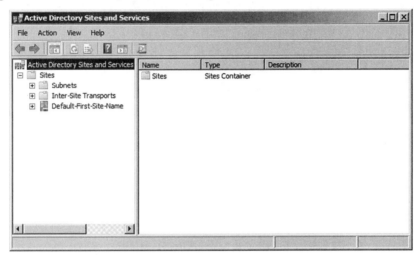

Figure 4-1
The Active Directory Sites and Services console

4. Right-click the *Sites* folder and, from the context menu, select *New Site*. The New Object – Site dialog box appears.

5. In the Name text box, type **Boston**.

6. Select the DEFAULTIPSITELINK site link object and click *OK*. An Active Directory Domain Services message box appears, informing you of the remaining steps in the site configuration process.

7. Click *OK*. The message box clears.

8. Repeat steps 4 to 7 to create site objects for the following branch offices:
   - Cheyenne
   - Chicago
   - Dallas
   - Miami
   - Portland

9. Take a screen shot of the Active Directory Sites and Services console, showing the site objects you created, by pressing Ctrl+Prt Scr, and then paste the resulting image into the lab04_worksheet file in the page provided by pressing Ctrl+V.

10. Leave the console open for the next exercise.

Exercise 4.2	Creating Subnets
Overview	Subnet objects associate sites with specific TCP/IP networks. In Create subnet objects for the each of the sites you created earlier.
Completion time	15 minutes

1. In the Active Directory Sites and Services console, right-click the *Subnets* container and, from the context menu, select *New Subnet*. The New Object – Subnet dialog box appears, as shown in Figure 4-2.

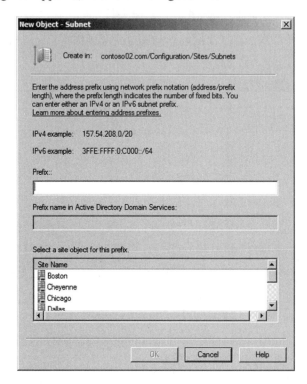

Figure 4-2
The New Object – Subnet dialog box

2. In the Prefix text box, type **10.1.*xx*.0/24**, where *xx* is the number that your instructor has assigned to your server.

3. In the Select a site object for this prefix list, select **Boston** and click *OK*. The new subnet appears beneath the Subnets container.

Question 1	*What is the primary benefit of creating subnet objects for the network administrator?*

4.   Repeat steps 1 to 3 to create five additional subnets, using the following values:

   - Cheyenne – 10.2.*xx*.0/24
   - Chicago – 10.3.*xx*.0/24
   - Dallas – 10.4.*xx*.0/24
   - Miami – 10.5.*xx*.0/24
   - Portland – 10.6.*xx*.0/24

Question 2	*What is the primary benefit of creating subnet objects for the network user?*

5.   Right-click the *Default-First-Site-Name site* and, from the context menu, select *Rename*. Type **Memphis** and press *Enter*. The site object is renamed.

6.   Leave the console open for the next exercise.

Exercise 4.3	Drawing a Site Diagram
Overview	The lab network will use a full-mesh replication topology, meaning that each pair of sites will have its own connection. Draw a diagram of the connections among the various sites.
Completion time	15 minutes

1.   On the map shown in Figure 4-3, draw a diagram that shows the links between the sites you created earlier:

Figure 4-3
Diagram of lab network sites

Exercise 4.4	Creating Site Link Objects
Overview	Site link objects represent connections between sites running at dofferent speeds. Create site links for each of the pairs of sites in the enterprise.
Completion time	15 minutes

1. In the Active Directory Sites and Services console, expand the Inter-Site Transports container and select the IP container.

2. Right-click the *IP container* and, from the context menu, select *New Site Link*. The New Object – Site Link dialog box appears, as shown in Figure 4-4.

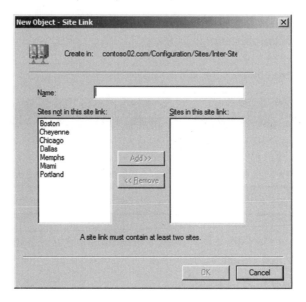

Figure 4-4
The New Object – Site Link dialog box

3. In the name text box, type **Memphis-Boston.**

4. In the Sites not in this link list, select *Memphis* and *Boston* and click *Add*. Memphis and Boston appear in the Sites in this site link list.

5. Click *OK*. The new site link object appears in the IP container.

6. Repeat steps 2 to 5 to create the following additional site link objects:

   - Memphis – Cheyenne
   - Memphis – Chicago
   - Memphis – Dallas
   - Memphis – Miami
   - Memphis – Portland
   - Chicago – Boston

- Chicago – Cheyenne
- Chicago – Dallas
- Chicago – Miami
- Chicago – Portland
- Boston – Cheyenne
- Boston – Dallas
- Boston – Miami
- Boston – Portland
- Portland – Cheyenne
- Portland – Dallas
- Portland – Miami
- Miami – Cheyenne
- Miami – Dallas
- Dallas – Cheyenne

Question 3	*Why might it be necessary to create individual site link objects for each pair of sites, even though some of the pairs run at the same speeds?*

7. Right-click the *DEFAULTIPSITELINK* object and, from the context menu, select *Delete*. An Active Directory Domain Services message box appears, confirming your action.

8. Click *Yes*. The DEFAULTIPSITELINK object is deleted.

9. Take a screen shot of the Active Directory Sites and Services console, showing the site link objects you created, by pressing Ctrl+Prt Scr, and then paste the resulting image into the Lab04_worksheet file in the page provided by pressing Ctrl+V.

10. Leave the console open for the next exercise.

Exercise 4.5	Calculating Site Link Costs
Overview	The cost of a site link is based on its speed and its available bandwidth. Calculate the cost values you will use to configure the replication between sites.
Completion time	15 minutes

1. In Table 4-2, calculate the net speed for each of the site links by multiplying the site link speed by the percentage of available bandwidth, rounding the answers to the nearest one.

Table 4-2
Site Link Replication Statistics

Site link	Site link speed	Available bandwidth	Net speed	Site cost
Memphis – Boston	128 Kbps	80%		
Memphis – Cheyenne	256 Kbps	50%		
Memphis – Chicago	128 Kbps	75%		
Memphis – Dallas	128 Kbps	60%		
Memphis – Miami	128 Kbps	75%		
Memphis – Portland	128 Kbps	30%		
Chicago – Boston	1.544 Mbps	40%		
Chicago – Cheyenne	256 Kbps	50%		
Chicago – Dallas	512 Kbps	30%		
Chicago – Miami	1.544 Mbps	60%		
Chicago – Portland	128 Kbps	40%		
Boston – Cheyenne	256 Kbps	70%		
Boston – Dallas	512 Kbps	80%		
Boston – Miami	1.544 Mbps	60%		
Boston – Portland	64 Kbps	75%		
Portland – Cheyenne	256 Kbps	40%		
Portland – Dallas	64 Kbps	20%		
Portland – Miami	512 Kbps	50%		
Miami – Cheyenne	256 Kbps	60%		
Miami – Dallas	512 Kbps	20%		
Dallas – Cheyenne	256 Kbps	80%		

2.   Calculate a site cost for each site link. One efficient way of doing this is to subtract the net speed you calculated from 1000.

3.   Leave the Active Directory Sites and Services console open for the next exercise.

Exercise 4.6	Configuring Site Replication
Overview	The cost of a site link is based on its speed and its available bandwidth. Calculate the cost values you will use to configure the replication between sites.
Completion time	15 minutes

1. In the Active Directory Sites and Services console, right-click the first site in the IP container and, from the context menu, select *Properties*. The Properties sheet for the site link appears, as shown in Figure 4-5.

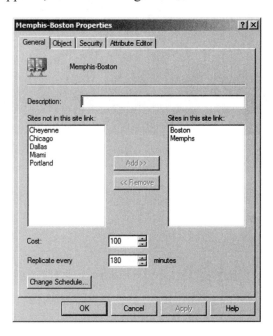

Figure 4-5
A site link's Properties sheet

2. Using the site cost figure you calculated for the site link in Exercise 4.5, set the value of the Cost spin box and click *OK*.

3. Repeat steps 1 to 2 to specify the site cost you calculated for each of the site link objects you created.

4. Take a screen shot of the Active Directory Sites and Services console, showing the site link objects you created and their costs, by pressing Ctrl+Prt Scr, and then paste the resulting image into the Lab04_worksheet file in the page provided by pressing Ctrl+V.

LAB 5
CREATING PASSWORD POLICIES

This lab contains the following exercises and activities:

BEFORE YOU BEGIN

The lab environment consists of student servers connected to a local area network, along with a classroom server that functions as the domain controller for a domain called contoso.com. Each student has his or her own server, which functions as a domain controller for a separate forest. Most of the exercises in this manual will require each student to work on his or her own domain controller in a separate Active Directory Domain Services domain.

> **NOTE**
>
> In the classroom lab environment, the instructor has assigned each server a number that the student will use to form the server's IP address, computer name, and domain name, as specified in Lab 1. This will keep each server in its own separate environment and prevent server interaction until it is specifically needed. You must complete Lab 1 before you proceed with the exercises in this lab.

In addition to the computers, you will also require the software listed in Table 5-1 to complete Lab 5.

Table 5-1
Software required for Lab 5

Software	Location
Lab 5 student worksheet	Lab05_worksheet.rtf (provided by instructor)

Working with Lab Worksheets

Each lab in this manual requires that you answer questions, shoot screen shots, and perform other activities that you will document in a worksheet named for the lab, such as Lab05_worksheet.rtf. Your instructor will provide you with access to the worksheets. It is recommended that you use a USB flash drive to store your worksheets, so you can submit them to your instructor for review. As you perform the exercises in each lab, open the appropriate worksheet file using WordPad, fill in the required information, and save the file to your flash drive.

SCENARIO

You are an enterprise administrator working in a lab environment where you are testing designs for the Windows Server 2008 R2 infrastructure services that your company will need for a new division it is deploying in the near future. In your current lab scenario, you are testing various Password and Account Lockout Policy settings, to determine which are most effective for your various types of users. You are also performing a trial deployment of fine-grained password policies, to determine if they can eliminate the need for separate domains.

After completing this lab, you will be able to:

- Create and deploy a GPO

- Configure Password Policy and Account Lockout Policy settings

- Configure fine-grained password policies

Estimated lab time: 55 minutes

Exercise 5.1	Creating a Group Policy Object
Overview	Create a new Group Policy object, with which you will deploy new Password Policy settings to your domain.
Completion time	5 minutes

1. Log on to your server using the **Administrator** account and the password **Pa$$w0rd**. The Initial Configuration Tasks window appears.

2. Click *Start*. Then click *Administrative Tools > Group Policy Management*. The Group Policy Management console appears.

3. Browse to the contoso*xx*.com domain, where *xx* is the number your instructor assigned to your server, as shown in Figure 5-1.

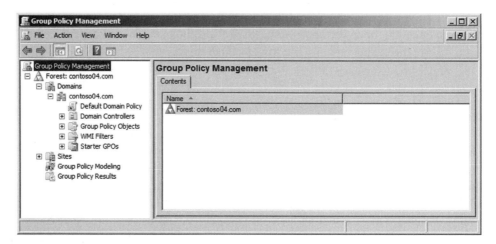

Figure 5-1
The Group Policy Management console

4. Right-click the Group Policy Objects container and, from the context menu, select *New*. The New GPO dialog box appears.

5. In the Name text box, type **Password Policies** and click *OK*. The new GPO appears in the Group Policy Objects container.

6. Leave the Group Policy Management console open for the next exercise.

Exercise 5.2	Modifying Password Policy Settings
Overview	Edit the GPO you created in Exercise 5.1 by modifying its Password Policy settings.
Completion time	20 minutes

1. In the Group Policy Management console, right-click the *Password Policies* GPO you created in Exercise 5.1 and, from the context menu, select *Edit*. The Group Policy Management Editor console appears

2. Browse to the Computer Configuration\Policies\Windows Settings\Security Settings\Account Policies\Password Policy container, as shown in Figure 5-2.

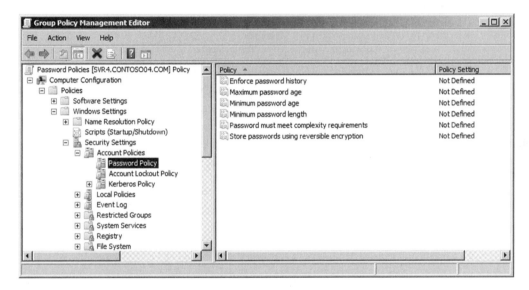

Figure 5-2
The Password Policy container in the Group Policy Management Editor console

3. Double-click the *Maximum password age* policy. The Maximum Password Age Properties sheet appears.

4. Select the *Define this policy setting* check box.

5. Set the spin-box value to *7 days* and click *OK*.

Question 1	*How does reducing the Maximum Password Age value increase the security of the network?*

6.   Configure the remaining Password Policy settings, using the values shown in Table 5-2.

Table 5-2
Password Policy Settings

Password Policy	Policy Value
Enforce password history	24 passwords remembered
Maximum password age	7 days
Minimum password age	6 days
Minimum password length	8 characters
Password must meet complexity requirements	Enabled
Store passwords using reversible encryption	Disabled

Question 2	*Would reducing the value of the Enforce Password History policy increase or decrease the security of the network? Explain your answer.*

Question 3	*Does increasing the Minimum Password Age value from 0 to 6 days decrease or increase the security of the network? Explain why.*

7.   Take a screen shot of the Group Policy Management Editor console, showing the Password Policy settings you just configured, by pressing Ctrl+Prt Scr, and then paste the resulting image into the Lab05_worksheet file in the page provided by pressing Ctrl+V.

8.   Browse to the Computer Configuration\Policies\Windows Settings\Security Settings\Account Policies\Account Lockout Policy container.

9.   Configure the Account Lockout Policy settings, using the values shown in Table 5-3.

Table 5-3
Account Lockout Policy Settings

Account Lockout Policy	Policy Value
Account lockout duration	0 minutes
Account lockout threshold	3 invalid logon attempts
Reset account lockout after	60 minutes

10.   Close the Group Policy Management Editor console.

11.   Leave the Group Policy Management console open for the next exercise.

Exercise 5.3	Linking a GPO
Overview	Edit the GPO you created in Exercise 5.1 by modifying its Password Policy settings.
Completion time	5 minutes

1.   In the Group Policy Management console, right-click the *contosoxx.com domain,* where *xx* is the number your instructor assigned to your server, and, in the context menu, select *Link an Existing GPO.* The Select GPO dialog box appears, as shown in Figure 5-3.

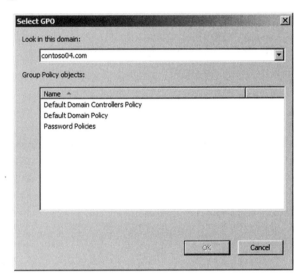

Figure 5-3
The Select GPO dialog box

2.   In the Group Policy objects list, select *Password Policies* and click *OK.* The Password Policies GPO appears in the Linked Group Policy Objects list for the domain.

3.   Take a screen shot of the Group Policy Management console, showing the Group Policy objects linked to your domain, by pressing Ctrl+Prt Scr, and then paste the resulting image into the Lab05_worksheet file in the page provided by pressing Ctrl+V.

Question 4	*In the Linked Group Policy Object list as it appears when you add the Password Policies GPO you created, which GPO takes precedence in the domain configuration? Explain why.*

4.   Close the Group Policy Management console.

5. Leave the server logged on for the next exercise.

Exercise 5.4	Creating a Password Settings Object
Overview	Beginning in Windows Server 2008, it is possible to create fine-grained password policies and apply them to groups, rather than create separate domains. Create a password settings object (PSO) containing fine-grained password policies.
Completion time	15 minutes

1. Click *Start*. Then click *Administrative Tools > ADSI Edit*. The ADSI Edit console appears.

2. Right-click the *ADSI Edit* node and, in the context menu, select *Connect to*. The Connection Settings dialog box appears.

3. In the Name text box, type **contoso*xx*.com**, where *xx* is the number your instructor assigned to your server, and click *OK*. The contosoxx.com domain appears beneath the ADSI Edit node.

4. Browse to the contoso*xx*.com\DC=contoso*xx*,DC=com\CN=System container, as shown in Figure 5-4.

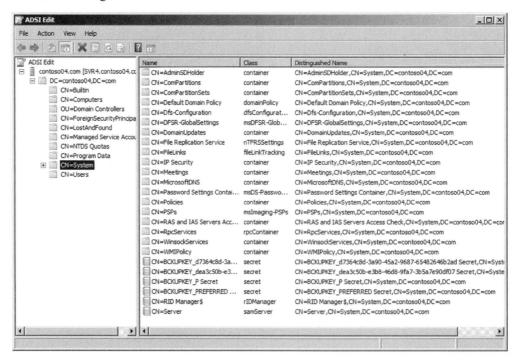

Figure 5-4
The ADSI Edit console

5. Right-click the *CN=Password Settings Container* object and, from the context menu, select *New > Object*. The Create Object Wizard appears.

6. Leave the msDS-PasswordSettings class selected and click *Next*. The *Common Name* page appears.

7. In the Value text box, type **PasswordPolicies1** and click *Next*. The *Password Settings Precedence* page appears.

8. In the Value text box, type **10** and click *Next*. The *Password reversible encryption status for user accounts* page appears.

9. In the Value text box, type **FALSE** and click *Next*. The *Password History Length for user accounts* page appears.

10. In the Value text box, type **24** and click *Next*. The *Password complexity status for user accounts* page appears.

11. In the Value text box, type **TRUE** and click *Next*. The *Minimum Password Length for user accounts* page appears.

12. In the Value text box, type **8** and click *Next*. The *Minimum Password Age for user accounts* page appears.

13. In the Value text box, type **6:00:00:00** and click *Next*. The *Maximum Password Age for user accounts* page appears.

> **NOTE** *Time intervals in a PSO are expressed in days, hours, minutes, and seconds, using the following format: d:hh:mm:ss.*

14. In the Value text box, type **7:00:00:00** and click *Next*. The *Lockout threshold for lockout of user accounts* page appears.

15. In the Value text box, type **3** and click *Next*. The *Observation window for lockout of user accounts* page appears.

16. In the Value text box, type **0:01:00:00** and click *Next*. The *Lockout duration for locked out user accounts* page appears.

17. In the Value text box, type **60** and click *Next*. The final page appears.

18. Click *Finish*. The wizard creates the PSO object.

19. Take a screen shot of the ADSI Edit console, showing the PSO object you just created, by pressing Ctrl+Prt Scr, and then paste the resulting image into the Lab05_worksheet file in the page provided by pressing Ctrl+V.

20. Close the ADSI Edit console.

21. Leave the server logged on for the next exercise.

Exercise 5.5	Linking a PSO to a Group
Overview	Once you have created a PSO and configured its attributes, you can deploy it on the network by associating it with a group object.
Completion time	10 minutes

1. Click *Start*. Then click *Administrative Tools > Active Directory Users and Computers*. The Active Directory Users and Computers console appears.

2. Click *View > Advanced Features*. The console displays expands to include additional objects.

3. Browse to the contosoxx.com\System\Password Settings Container object.

4. Double-click the P*asswordPolicies1* object you created. The PasswordPolicies1 Properties sheet appears.

5. Click the Attribute Editor tab, as shown in Figure 5-5.

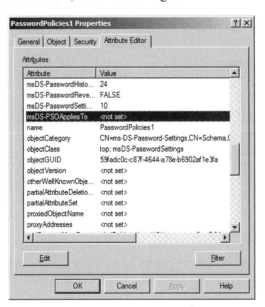

Figure 5-5
The Attribute Editor tab of the PasswordPolicies1
Properties sheet

6. Scroll down and select the *msDS-PSOAppliesTo* attribute and click *Edit*. The Multi-valued Distinguished Name with Security Principal Editor dialog box appears.

7. Click *Add Windows Account*. The Select Users, Computers, or Groups dialog box appears.

8. In the Enter the object names to select box, type **Backup Operators** and click *OK*. The group appears in the values list of the Multi-valued Distinguished Name with Security Principal Editor dialog box.

9. Take a screen shot of the Multi-valued Distinguished Name with Security Principal Editor dialog box, showing the group you just added, by pressing Ctrl+Prt Scr, and then paste the resulting image into the Lab05_worksheet file in the page provided by pressing Ctrl+V.

10. Click *OK* to close the Multi-valued Distinguished Name with Security Principal Editor dialog box.

11. Click *OK* to close the PasswordPolicies1 Properties sheet.

12. Close the Active Directory Users and Computers console.

13. Log off of the computer.

LAB 6
USING ACTIVE DIRECTORY MIGRATION TOOL

This lab contains the following exercises and activities:

BEFORE YOU BEGIN

The lab environment consists of student servers connected to a local area network, along with a classroom server that functions as the domain controller for a domain called contoso.com. Each student has his or her own server, which functions as a domain controller for a separate forest. Most of the exercises in this manual will require each student to work on his or her own domain controller in a separate Active Directory Domain Services domain.

NOTE	In the classroom lab environment, the instructor originally assigned each server a number that the student used to form the server's IP address, computer name, and domain name, as specified in Lab 1. This kept each server in its own separate environment and prevented server interaction. For this lab, however, interaction between servers in different forests is needed, so you will begin by reconfiguring your server's TCP/IP settings, to place your server on a common classroom subnet. You must complete Exercise 6.1 before you proceed to the other exercises.

In addition to the computers, you will also require the software listed in Table 6-1 to complete Lab 6.

Table 6-1
Software required for Lab 6

Software	Location
SQL Server 2005 Express SP3	http://www.microsoft.com/downloads/en/details.aspx?FamilyID=3181842a-4090-4431-acdd-9a1c832e65a6
Active Directory Migration Tool 3.2	http://www.microsoft.com/downloads/details.aspx?familyid=20C0DB45-DB16-4D10-99F2-539B7277CCDB&displaylang=en
Lab 6 student worksheet	Lab06_worksheet.rtf (provided by instructor)

NOTE	Internet URLs often change, so the addresses in the table may be different by the time you read this. If this is the case, run a search at http://www.microsoft.com/downloads or check with your instructor for the correct URLs.

NOTE	For this application, do not use SQL Server Express 2008 because there is a known issue when the database engine is installed on a domain controller.

Working with Lab Worksheets

Each lab in this manual requires that you answer questions, shoot screen shots, and perform other activities that you will document in a worksheet named for the lab, such as Lab06_worksheet.rtf. Your instructor will provide you with access to the worksheets. It is recommended that you use a USB flash drive to store your worksheets, so you can submit them to your instructor for review. As you perform the exercises in each lab, open the appropriate worksheet file using WordPad, fill in the required information, and save the file to your flash drive.

SCENARIO

You are an enterprise administrator working in a lab environment where you are testing designs for the Windows Server 2008 R2 infrastructure services that your company will need for a new division it is deploying in the near future. In your current lab scenario, you are practicing the process of migrating AD DS objects between domains in different forests, using the Microsoft Active Directory Migration Tool.

After completing this lab, you will be able to:

- Install SQL Server Express

- Install Active Directory Migration Tool

- Migrate group objects

- Migrate user objects

Estimated lab time: 100 minutes

Exercise 6.1	Reconfiguring TCP/IP
Overview	To accommodate the installation of SQL Server Express and the Active Directory Migration Tool, you must modify your server's IP address so that you can access the Internet.
Completion time	5 minutes

1. Log on to your server using the **Administrator** account and the password **Pa$$w0rd**. The Initial Configuration Tasks window appears.

2. In the Initial Configuration Tasks window, click *Configure networking*. The Network Connections window appears.

3. Right-click the *Local Area Connection* icon and, from the context menu, select *Properties*. The Local Area Connection Properties sheet appears.

4. Select *Internet Protocol Version 4 (TCP/IPv4)* and click *Properties*. The Internet Protocol Version 4 (TCP/IPv4) Properties sheet appears.

5. In the IP address text box, type **10.0.0.xx**, where *xx* is the number your instructor assigned to your server.

6. In the Subnet mask text box, type **255.255.255.0**.

7. In the Default gateway text box, type **10.0.0.1.**

8. Leave the Preferred DNS server text box set to **127.0.0.1**.

9.   Click *OK* to close the Internet Protocol Version 4 (TCP/IPv4) Properties sheet.

10. Click *OK* to close the Local Area Connection Properties sheet.

11. Close the Network Connections window.

12. Leave the server logged on for the next exercise.

Exercise 6.2	Installing SQL Server Express
Overview	Install the SQL Server Express software needed to support the Active Directory Migration Tool.
Completion time	15 minutes

1.   Click *Start*. Then click *Internet Explorer*. The Internet Explorer window appears.

2.   Download the 64-bit version of SQL Server Express 2005 SP3 from the URL listed in Table 6-1 and save it to your local drive.

3.   Execute the SQLEXPR.exe file you downloaded. The executable expands the files in the archive and loads the Microsoft SQL Server 2005 Setup Wizard, displaying the *End User License Agreement* page.

4.   Select the I accept the licensing terms and conditions check box and click *Next*. The *Installing Prerequisites* page appears.

5.   Click *Install*. The wizard installs the required components.

6.   Click *Next*. The *System Configuration Check* page appears briefly, and then the Microsoft SQL Server Installation Wizard appears.

7.   Click *Next* to bypass the *Welcome* page. The *System Configuration Check* page appears.

8.   Click *Next*, ignoring any Warning test results. The *Registration Information* page appears.

9.   Click *Next* to accept the default values. The *Feature Selection* page appears, as shown in Figure 6-1.

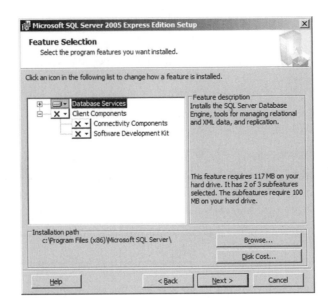

Figure 6-1
The *Feature Selection* page of the Microsoft SQL
Server Installation Wizard

10. Click *Next* to accept the default selections. The *Authentication Mode* page
    appears.

11. Click *Next* to accept the defaults. The *Configuration Options* page appears.

12. Click *Next*. The *Error and Usage Report Settings* page appears.

13. Click *Next*. The *Ready to Install* page appears.

14. Click *Install*. The *Setup Progress* page appears as the wizard installs the
    software.

15. Click *Next*. The *Completing Microsoft SQL Server 2005 Setup* page appears.

16. Click *Finish*. The Wizard closes.

17. Leave the server logged on for the next exercise.

Exercise 6.3	Installing Active Directory Migration Tool
Overview	Install the Active Directory Migration Tool.
Completion time	15 minutes

1. In Internet Explorer, download the Active Directory Migration Tool from the
   URL listed in Table 6-1 and save it to your local drive.

2. Execute the Admtsetup32.exe file you downloaded. The Active Directory
   Migration Tool Installation Wizard appears.

3. Click *Next* to bypass the *Welcome* page. The *License Agreement* page appears.

4. Select the *I Agree* option and click *Next*. The *Customer Experience Improvement Program* page appears.

5. Select the *I don't want to join the program at this time* option and click *Next*. The *Database Selection* page appears, as shown in Figure 6-2.

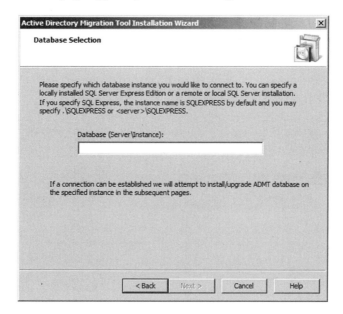

Figure 6-2
The *Database Selection* page

6. In the Database (Server\Instance) text box, type **.\SQLEXPRESS** and click *Next*. The *Configuring Components* page appears as the wizard installs ADMT. The *Database Import* page appears.

7. Click *Next* with the default No option selected. The *Active Directory Migration Tool Version 3.2 has been successfully installed* page appears.

8. Take a screen shot of the *Active Directory Migration Tool Version 3.2 has been successfully installed* page, by pressing Ctrl+Prt Scr, and then paste the resulting image into the Lab06_worksheet file in the page provided by pressing Ctrl+V.

9. Click *Finish*. The wizard closes.

10. Leave the server logged on for the next exercise.

Exercise 6.4	Migrating Groups
Overview	Use the Active Directory Migration Tool to copy groups between forests.
Completion time	15 minutes

NOTE	*Before you begin this exercise, select another student in the classroom to function as your partner. You will use each other's servers to perform AD DS object migrations.*

---

1. Click *Start*. Then click *Administration Tools > Active Directory Migration Tool*. The Active Directory Migration Tool console appears.

2. Right-click the *Active Directory Migration Tool* container and, from the context menu, select Group Account Migration Wizard. The Group Account Migration Wizard appears.

3. Click *Next* to bypass the *Welcome* page. The *Domain Selection* page appears, as shown in Figure 6-3.

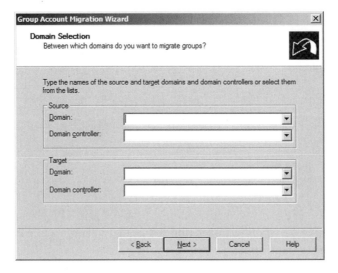

Figure 6-3
The *Domain Selection* page

4. In the Source box, in the Domain text box, type the name of your partner's domain – **contosoxx.com**, where *xx* is the number your instructor assigned to your partner's computer.

5. In the Source box, in the Domain Controller drop-down list, select *<Any domain controller>*.

6. In the Target box, in the Domain text box, type the name of your domain – **contosoxx.com**, where *xx* is the number your instructor assigned to your computer.

7. In the Target box, in the Domain Controller drop-down list, select your server – *\\SVRxx.contosoxx.com,* where *xx* is the number your instructor assigned to your computer.

8. Click *Next*. An Error message box appears, stating that the specified domain does not exist or could not be contacted.

Question 1	Which domain could not be contacted?

Question 2	Why was the Active Directory Migration Tool unable to contact the other domain?

9. Take a screen shot of the error message box, by pressing Ctrl+Prt Scr, and then paste the resulting image into the Lab06_worksheet file in the page provided by pressing Ctrl+V.

10. Click *OK* to close the error message box.

11. Click *Cancel* to close the Group Account Migration Wizard. A Cancel? Message box appears.

12. Click *Yes*. The wizard closes.

13. Close the Active Directory Migration Tool console.

14. Leave the server logged on for the next exercise.

Exercise 6.5	Preparing to Run ADMT
Overview	Configure the DNS service on your server to locate your partner's domain, from which you will copy objects using the Active Directory Migration Tool.
Completion time	10 minutes

1. Click *Start*. Then click *Administrative Tools > DNS*. The DNS Manager console appears.

2. Expand the Forward Lookup Zones container.

3. Right-click the zone representing your domain – *contosoxx.com,* where *xx* is the number your instructor assigned to your computer – and, from the context menu, select *Properties*. The Properties sheet for the zone appears.

4. Select the *Zone Transfers* tab.

5. Select the *Allow zone transfers* check box and, leaving the *To any server* option selected, click *OK*.

6. Right-click the *Forward Lookup Zones* container and, from the context menu, select *New Zone*. The New Zone Wizard appears.

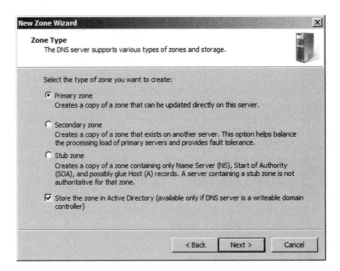

Figure 6-4
The *Zone Type* page

7. Click *Next* to bypass the *Welcome* page. The *Zone Type* page appears, as shown in Figure 6-4.

8. Select the Secondary zone option and click *Next*. The *Zone Name* page appears.

Question 3	Why is the Store the zone in Active Directory check box grayed out when you select the Secondary zone option?

9. In the Zone name text box, type the name of your partner's domain—**contoso*xx*.com**, where *xx* is the number your instructor assigned to your partner's computer—and click *Next*. The *Master DNS Servers* page appears.

10. In the Master Servers list type **10.0.0.*xx*,** where *xx* is the number your instructor assigned to your partner's computer, and press Enter. The wizard validates the IP address and adds it to the list.

11. Take a screen shot of the *Master DNS Servers* page by pressing Ctrl+Prt Scr, and then paste the resulting image into the Lab06_worksheet file in the page provided by pressing Ctrl+V.

12. Click *Next*. The *Completing the New Zone Wizard* page appears.

13. Click *Finish*. The wizard closes.

14. Right-click the new zone you just created and, from the context menu, select *Transfer from Master*.

NOTE	*It might take several minutes for the zone transfer from your partner's DNS server to your to complete. Select Action > Reload to update the display.*

15.   Close the DNS Manager console.

16.   Leave the server logged on for the next exercise.

Exercise 6.6	Migrating Groups (Attempt 2)
Overview	With the DNS service updated, you should now be able to run the Active Directory Migration Tool and copy objects from one domain to the other.
Completion time	15 minutes

1.   Click *Start*. Then click *Administration Tools > Active Directory Migration Tool*. The Active Directory Migration Tool console appears.

2.   Right-click the *Active Directory Migration Tool* container and, from the context menu, select Group Account Migration Wizard. The Group Account Migration Wizard appears.

3.   Click *Next* to bypass the *Welcome* page. The *Domain Selection* page appears.

4.   In the Source box in the Domain text box, type the name of your partner's domain—**contoso*xx*.com**, where *xx* is the number your instructor assigned to your partner's computer.

5.   In the Source box, in the Domain Controller drop-down list, select <Any domain controller>.

6.   In the Target box, in the Domain text box, type the name of your domain—**contoso*xx*.com**, where *xx* is the number your instructor assigned to your computer.

7.   In the Target box, in the Domain Controller drop-down list, select your server—\\SVR*xx*.contoso*xx*.com, where *xx* is the number your instructor assigned to your computer.

8.   Click *Next*. The *Group Selection Option* page appears.

9. Leave the Select groups from domain option selected and click *Next*. The *Group Selection* page appears, as shown in Figure 6-5.

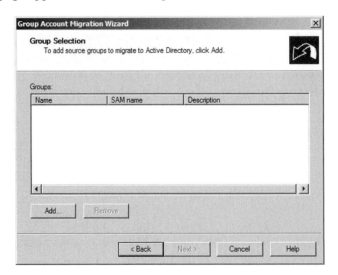

Figure 6-5
The *Group Selection* page

10. Click *Add*. The Select Groups dialog box appears.

11. In the Enter the object names to select box, type **Remote Desktop Users** and click *OK*. The group appears on the *Group Selection* page.

12. Click *Next*. The *Organizational Unit Selection* page appears.

13. Click *Browse*. The *Browse for Container* page appears.

14. Select the Users OU and click *OK*. The LDAP address for the OU appears in the *Organizational Unit Selection* page.

15. Click *Next*. The *Group Options* page appears.

16. Clear the Copy group members check box and click *Next*. The *Object Property Exclusion* page appears.

17. Click *Next* to accept the default settings. The *Conflict Management* page appears.

18. Click *Next* to accept the default settings. The Completing the Group Account Migration Wizard appears.

19. Click *Finish*. The *Migration Progress* page appears as the wizard copies the selected group objects.

20. Take a screen shot of the *Migration Progress* page, by pressing Ctrl+Prt Scr, and then paste the resulting image into the Lab06_worksheet file in the page provided by pressing Ctrl+V.

21. Click *Close*. The wizard closes.

22. Leave the Active Directory Migration Tool logged on for the next exercise.

Exercise 6.7	Creating a User Account
Overview	Before you can migrate a user object, you must create a user account on your lab server.
Completion time	5 minutes

1. Click *Start*. Then click *Administration Tools > Active Directory Users and Computers*. The Active Directory Users and Computers console appears.

2. Expand the contoso*xx*.com container, where *xx* is the number your instructor assigned to your computer.

3. Right-click the *Users* container and, from the context menu, select New > User. The New Object – User Wizard appears.

4. In the Full name field, type **Student*xx***, where *xx* is the number your instructor assigned to your computer.

5. In the User logon name text box, type **student*xx*** and click *Next*.

6. In the Password and Confirm password text boxes, type **Pa$$w0rd**.

7. Clear the User must change password at next logon check box.

8. Select the Password never expires check box and click *Next*.

9. Click *Finish*. The wizard creates the user account.

10. Close the Active Directory Users and Computers console.

Exercise 6.8	Migrating Users
Overview	Having migrated group objects, you can now proceed to migrate users.
Completion time	15 minutes

1. In the Active Directory Migration Tool console, right-click the Active Directory Migration Tool container and, from the context menu, select User Account Migration Wizard. The User Account Migration Wizard appears.

2. Click *Next* to bypass the *Welcome* page. The *Domain Selection* page appears.

3. In the Source box in the Domain text box, type the name of your partner's domain—**contoso*xx*.com**, where *xx* is the number your instructor assigned to your partner's computer.

4. In the Source box, in the Domain Controller drop-down list, select <Any domain controller>.

5. In the Target box, in the Domain text box, type the name of your domain—**contoso*xx*.com**, where *xx* is the number your instructor assigned to your computer.

6. In the Target box, in the Domain Controller drop-down list, select your server—\\SVR*xx*.contoso*xx*.com, where *xx* is the number your instructor assigned to your computer.

7. Click *Next*. The *User Selection Option* page appears.

8. Leave the Select users from domain option selected and click *Next*. The *User Selection* page appears.

NOTE	*Make sure that your partner has completed Exercise 6.7 before you proceed with the next step.*

9. Click *Add*. The Select Users dialog box appears.

10. In the Enter the object names to select box, type **Student*xx***, where *xx* is the number your instructor assigned to your partner's computer, and click *OK*. The user appears on *the User Selection* page.

11. Click *Next*. The *Organizational Unit Selection* page appears.

12. Click *Browse*. The *Browse for Container* page appears.

13. Select the Users OU and click *OK*. The LDAP address for the OU appears in the *Organizational Unit Selection* page.

14. Click *Next*. The *Password Options* page appears.

15. Select the Migrate passwords option and click *Next*. An Error message box appears, as shown in Figure 6-6, stating that the wizard is unable to establish a session with the password export server.

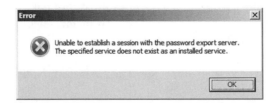

Figure 6-6
The Error message box

Question 4	What must you do for the Active Directory Migration Tool to be able to migrate passwords along with user accounts?

16. Click *OK* to close the Error message box.

17. Select the Generate complex passwords option and click *Next*. The *Account Transition Options* page appears.

18. Click *Next* to accept the default settings. The *User Options* page appears.

19. Click *Next* to accept the default settings. The *Object Property Exclusion* page appears.

20. Click *Next* to accept the default settings. The *Conflict Management* page appears.

21. Cllick *Next* to accept the default settings. The Completing the Group Account Migration Wizard appears.

22. Click *Finish*. The *Migration Progress* page appears as the wizard copies the selected group objects.

23. Click *Close*. The wizard closes.

24. Close the Active Directory Migration Tool.

Exercise 6.9	Restoring TCP/IP Settings
Overview	Once you have completed your work with the Active Directory Migration Tool, you can return your server back to its original TCP/IP configuration.
Completion time	5 minutes

1. In the Initial Configuration Tasks window, click *Configure networking*. The Network Connections window appears.

2. Right-click the *Local Area Connection* icon and, from the context menu, select Properties. The Local Area Connection Properties sheet appears.

3. Select Internet Protocol Version 4 (TCP/IPv4) and click *Properties*. The Internet Protocol Version 4 (TCP/IPv4) Properties sheet appears.

4. In the IP address text box, type **10.0.xx.1**, where *xx* is the number your instructor assigned to your server.

5. In the Subnet mask text box, type **255.255.255.0**.

6. In the Default gateway text box, remove the current setting and leave the box blank.

7. Leave the Preferred DNS server text box set to 127.0.0.1.

8. Click *OK* to close the Internet Protocol Version 4 (TCP/IPv4) Properties sheet.

9. Click *OK* to close the Local Area Connection Properties sheet.

10. Close the Network Connections window.

11. Log off of the server.

LAB 7
USING BRANCH OFFICE TECHNOLOGIES

This lab contains the following exercises and activities:

Exercise 7.1   Creating Branch Office OUs

Exercise 7.2   Creating Branch Office Managers

Exercise 7.3   Delegating Control to the Phoenix Office

Exercise 7.4   Delegating Control to the Tucson Office

Exercise 7.5   Delegating Control to the Tempe Office

Exercise 7.6   Creating a BranchCache Content Server GPO

Exercise 7.7   Creating a BranchCache Client GPO

BEFORE YOU BEGIN

The lab environment consists of student servers connected to a local area network, along with a classroom server that functions as the domain controller for a domain called contoso.com. Each student has his or her own server, which functions as a domain controller for a separate forest. Most of the exercises in this manual will require each student to work on his or her own domain controller in a separate Active Directory Domain Services domain.

> NOTE
>
> *In the classroom lab environment, the instructor has assigned each server a number that the student will use to form the server's IP address, computer name, and domain name, as specified in Lab 1. This will keep each server in its own separate environment and prevent server interaction until it is specifically needed. You must complete Lab 1 before you proceed with the exercises in this lab.*

In addition to the computers, you will also require the software listed in Table 7-1 to complete Lab 7.

Table 7-1
Software required for Lab 7

Software	Location
Lab 7 student worksheet	Lab07_worksheet.rtf (provided by instructor)

Working with Lab Worksheets

Each lab in this manual requires that you answer questions, shoot screen shots, and perform other activities that you will document in a worksheet named for the lab, such as Lab07_worksheet.rtf. Your instructor will provide you with access to the worksheets. It is recommended that you use a USB flash drive to store your worksheets, so you can submit them to your instructor for review. As you perform the exercises in each lab, open the appropriate worksheet file using WordPad, fill in the required information, and save the file to your flash drive.

SCENARIO

Contoso, Ltd. is opening three branch offices in Arizona, in the cities of Tempe Tucson, and Phoenix. The offices vary in size and in the administrative capabilities of the people in charge of them. The Phoenix office is the largest, with 125 users and a staff of full-time network administrators. The Tucson office has 35 users and one network administrator. The Tempe office has only five users, none of whom have any formal training in network administration. You have been appointed administrator of the branch offices, working out of the company headquarters. You want the management personnel at the branch offices to perform as many of the basic administrative tasks as they can, but you don't want to give them capabilities that they are not qualified to use. You have also been instructed to create Group Policy objects that will configure the branch office computers to conserve bandwidth by using BranchCache.

After completing this lab, you will be able to:

- Use the Delegation of Control Wizard

- Configure BranchCache policies

Estimated lab time: 60 minutes

Exercise 7.1	Creating Branch Office OUs
Overview	Create organizational units for each of the three Arizona branch offices. By creating a parent OU called Branch Offices, you can exercise control over all three branches at once, if necessary.
Completion time	5 minutes

1. Log on to your server using the **Administrator** account and the password **Pa$$w0rd**. The Initial Configuration Tasks window appears.

2. Click *Start*. Then click *Administration Tools > Active Directory users and Computers*. The Active Directory Users and Computers console appears.

3. Browse to the contosoxx.com domain node.

4. Right-click the *contosoxx.com* domain and, from the context menu, select New > Organizational Unit. The New Object – Organizational Unit dialog box appears, as shown in Figure 7-1.

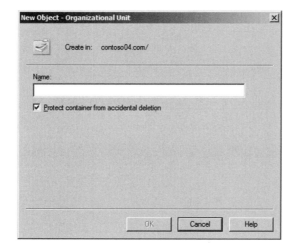

Figure 7-1
The New Object – Organizational Unit dialog box

5. In the Name text box, type **Branch Offices** and click *OK*. The new Branch Offices OU appears in the domain.

6. Right-click the *Branch offices OU* and, from the context menu, select New > Organizational Unit. The New Object – Organizational Unit dialog box appears.

7. In the Name text box, type **Phoenix** and click *OK*. The new Phoenix OU appears in the domain.

8. Repeat steps 6 and 7 to create two additional OUs in the Branch Offices OU, called Tempe and Tucson.

9.   Take a screen shot of the Active Directory Users and Computers console showing the OUs you created, by pressing Ctrl+Prt Scr, and then paste the resulting image into the Lab07_worksheet file in the page provided by pressing Ctrl+V.

10. Leave the Active Directory Users and Computers console open for the next exercise.

Exercise 7.2	Creating Branch Manager Groups
Overview	Create a group for each of the new OUs, into which you will later add the users who are the managers of each branch office.
Completion time	5 minutes

1.   In the Active Directory Users and Computers console, right-click the *Branch Offices OU* you created in Exercise 7.1 and, from the context menu, select New > Group. The New Object – Group dialog box appears, as shown in Figure 7-2.

Figure 7-2
The New Object – Group dialog box

2.   In the Group name text box, type **Branch Managers**.

3.   Leave the Global and Security options selected and click *OK*. The new group appears in the Branch Offices OU.

4.   Right-click the *Phoenix OU* you created and, from the context menu, select New > Group. The New Object – Group dialog box appears.

5.   In the Group name text box, type **Phoenix Managers** and click *OK*. The new group appears in the Phoenix OU.

6.   Repeat steps 4 and 5 to create two additional groups, called Tempe Managers and Tucson Managers, in the Tempe and Tucson OUs, respectively.

7. Leave the Active Directory Users and Computers console open for the next exercise.

Exercise 7.3	Delegating Control to the Phoenix Office
Overview	The Phoenix branch office is the largest of the three and has a full IT staff. You can therefore give them administrative autonomy over the entire Phoenix organizational unit. Use the Delegation of Control Wizard to provide the Phoenix Managers group with full control over the Phoenix OU.
Completion time	10 minutes

1. In the Active Directory Users and Computers console, right-click the *Phoenix OU* you created in Exercise 7.1 and, from the context menu, select Delegate Control. The Delegation of Control Wizard appears.

2. Click *Next* to bypass the *Welcome* page. The *Users or Groups* page appears.

3. Click *Add*. The Select Users, Computers, or Groups dialog box appears.

4. In the Enter the object names to select box, type **Phoenix Managers; Branch Managers** and click *OK*. The groups appear in the Selected users and groups list.

5. Click *Next*. The *Tasks to Delegate* page appears.

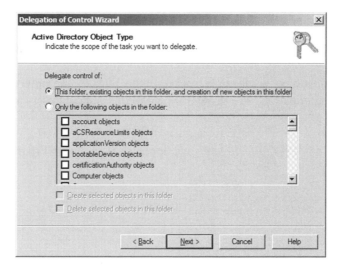

Figure 7-3
The *Active Directory Object Type* page of the Delegation of Control Wizard

6. Select the *Create a custom task to delegate* option and click *Next*. The *Active Directory Object Type* page appears, as shown in Figure 7-3.

7. Click *Next* to accept the default option. The *Permissions* page appears.

8. Select the Full Control check box.

9. Take a screen shot of the *Permissions* page showing the permissions you selected, by pressing Ctrl+Prt Scr, and then paste the resulting image into the Lab07_worksheet file in the page provided by pressing Ctrl+V.

10. Click *Next*. The *Completing the Delegation of Control Wizard* page appears.

11. Click *Finish*. The wizard closes.

12. Leave the Active Directory Users and Computers console open for the next exercise.

Exercise 7.4	Delegating Control to the Tucson Office
Overview	The Tucson branch office has a full-time network administrator who is capable of performing most of the everyday tasks required for upkeep of a branch-office organizational unit. Use the Delegation of Control Wizard to enable the Tucson branch office managers to perform a variety of user and group maintenance tasks.
Completion time	10 minutes

1. In the Active Directory Users and Computers console, right-click the *Tucson OU* you created in Exercise 7.1 and, from the context menu, select Delegate Control. The Delegation of Control Wizard appears.

2. Click *Next* to bypass the *Welcome* page. The *Users or Groups* page appears.

3. Click *Add*. The Select Users, Computers, or Groups dialog box appears.

4. In the Enter the object names to select box, type **Tucson Managers; Branch Managers** and click *OK*. The groups appear in the Selected users and groups list.

5. Click *Next*. The *Tasks to Delegate* page appears, as shown in Figure 7-4.

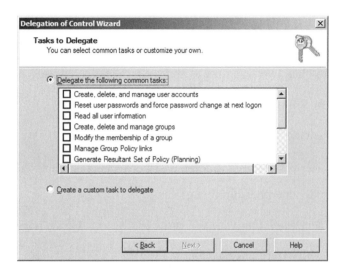

Figure 7-4
The *Tasks to Delegate* page of the Delegation of
Control Wizard

6. Select the following check boxes:

    *   Create, delete, and manage user accounts

    *   Reset user passwords and force password change at next logon

    *   Read all user information

    *   Create, delete, and manage groups

    *   Modify the membership of a group

7. Click *Next*. The *Completing the Delegation of Control Wizard* page appears.

8. Click *Finish*. The wizard closes.

9. Leave the Active Directory Users and Computers console open for the next exercise.

Exercise 7.5	Delegating Control to the Tempe Office
Overview	The Tempe branch office is the smallest of the three, and its manager has no network administration training or experience. However, you can supply the manager with instructions for performing a few basic tasks. Use the Delegation of Control Wizard to enable the Tempe branch office managers group to perform a minimal number of group maintenance tasks.
Completion time	10 minutes

1. In the Active Directory Users and Computers console, right-click the *Tempe OU* you created in Exercise 7.1 and, from the context menu, select Delegate Control. The Delegation of Control Wizard appears.

2. Click *Next* to bypass the *Welcome* page. The *Users or Groups* page appears.

3. Click *Add*. The Select Users, Computers, or Groups dialog box appears.

4. In the Enter the object names to select box, type **Tempe Managers; Branch Managers** and click *OK*. The groups appear in the Selected users and groups list.

5. Click *Next*. The *Tasks to Delegate* page appears.

6. Select the following check boxes:

   - Reset user passwords and force password change at next logon

   - Modify the membership of a group

7. Click *Next*. The *Completing the Delegation of Control Wizard* page appears.

8. Click *Finish*. The wizard closes.

9. Close the Active Directory Users and Computers console.

10. Leave the computer logged on for the next exercise.

Exercise 7.6	Creating a BranchCache Content Server GPO
Overview	Create a Group Policy object that contains the settings required by a computer that will funtion as a content server in a BranchCache installation.
Completion time	10 minutes

1. Click *Start*. Then click *Administrative Tools > Group Policy Management*. The Group Policy Management console appears.

2. Browse to the contoso*xx*.com domain, where *xx* is the number your instructor assigned to your server.

3. Right-click the *Group Policy Objects* container and, from the context menu, select New. The New GPO dialog box appears.

4. In the Name text box, type **BranchCache Content Servers** and click *OK*. The new GPO appears in the Group Policy Objects container.

5. Right-click the GPO you just created and, from the context menu, select Edit. The Group Policy Management Editor console appears.

6. Browse to the Computer Configuration\Policies\Administrative Templates\Network\Lanman Server container, as shown in Figure 7-5.

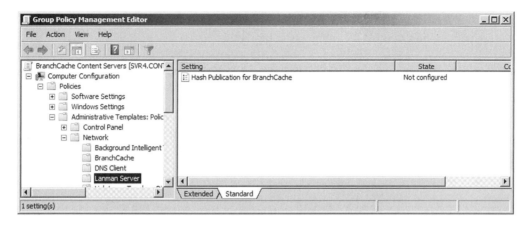

Figure 7-5
The Lanman Server container in a Group Policy object

7. Double-click the *Hash Publication for BranchCache* policy. The Hash Publication for BranchCache dialog box appears.

8. Select the Enabled option.

9. In the Hash publication actions drop-down list, select Allow hash publication only for shared folders on which BranchCache is enabled and click *OK*.

Question 1	Apart from applying this GPO, what else must administrators do to the content servers to enable BranchCache functionality?

10. Close the Group Policy Management Editor console.

11. Leave the computer logged on for the next exercise.

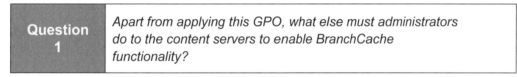

Exercise 7.7	Creating a BranchCache Client GPO
Overview	Create a Group Policy object that contains the settings required by a client computers in a BranchCache installation. The computers will cache their own server information, a configuration known as Distributed Cache mode.
Completion time	10 minutes

1. Click *Start*. Then click *Administrative Tools > Group Policy Management*. The Group Policy Management console appears.

2. Browse to the contoso*xx*.com domain, where *xx* is the number your instructor assigned to your server.

3. Right-click the *Group Policy Objects* container and, from the context menu, select New. The New GPO dialog box appears.

4. In the Name text box, type **BranchCache Clients** and click *OK*. The new GPO appears in the Group Policy Objects container.

5. Right-click the GPO you just created and, from the context menu, select Edit. The Group Policy Management Editor console appears.

6. Browse to the Computer Configuration\Policies\Administrative Templates\Network\BranchCache container, as shown in Figure 7-6.

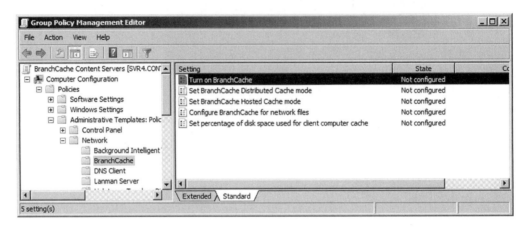

Figure 7-6
The BranchCache container in a Group Policy object

7. Double-click the *Turn on BranchCache* policy. The Turn on BranchCache dialog box appears.

8. Select the Enabled option and click *OK*.

9. Double-click the *Set BranchCache Distributed Cache mode* policy. The Set BranchCache Distributed Cache mode dialog box appears.

10. Select the Enabled option and click *OK*.

11. Close the Group Policy Management Editor console.

12. Close the Group Policy Management console.

13. Log off of the computer.

LAB 8
USING REMOTE DESKTOP SERVICES

This lab contains the following exercises and activities:

Exercise 8.1	Reconfiguring TCP/IP
Exercise 8.2	Installing the Remote Desktop Services Role
Exercise 8.3	Configuring RemoteApp Applications
Exercise 8.4	Creating an RDP File
Exercise 8.5	Creating RemoteApp RDP Files
Exercise 8.6	Creating a Share
Exercise 8.7	Using the Remote Desktop Connection Client
Exercise 8.8	Connecting Using RDP Files
Exercise 8.9	Connecting Using RD Web Access
Exercise 8.10	Restoring TCP/IP Settings

BEFORE YOU BEGIN

The lab environment consists of student servers connected to a local area network, along with a classroom server that functions as the domain controller for a domain called contoso.com. Each student has his or her own server, which functions as a domain controller for a separate forest. Most of the exercises in this manual will require each student to work on his or her own domain controller in a separate Active Directory Domain Services domain.

In addition to the computers, you will also require the software listed in Table 8-1 to complete Lab 8.

Table 8-1
Software required for Lab 8

Software	Location
Lab 8 student worksheet	Lab08_worksheet.rtf (provided by instructor)

Working with Lab Worksheets

Each lab in this manual requires that you answer questions, shoot screen shots, and perform other activities that you will document in a worksheet named for the lab, such as Lab08_worksheet.rtf. Your instructor will provide you with access to the worksheets. It is recommended that you use a USB flash drive to store your worksheets, so you can submit them to your instructor for review. As you perform the exercises in each lab, open the appropriate worksheet file using WordPad, fill in the required information, and save the file to your flash drive.

SCENARIO

You are an enterprise administrator working in a lab environment where you are testing designs for the Windows Server 2008 R2 infrastructure services that your company will need for a new division it is deploying in the near future. In your current lab scenario, you are evaluating the various Remote Desktop technologies provided with Windows Server 2008 R2, including the standard RDS desktops, RemoteApp, and Remote Desktop Web Access.

After completing this lab, you will be able to:

- Install and configure Remote Desktop Services

- Connect to an RDS server using multiple clients

Estimated lab time: 95 minutes

Exercise 8.1	Reconfiguring TCP/IP
Overview	To enable your server and your partner server to connect to each other using Remote Desktop Services, you must modify your server's IP address so that you can access the Internet.
Completion time	5 minutes

1. Log on to your server using the **Administrator** account and the password **Pa$$w0rd**. The Initial Configuration Tasks window appears.

2. In the Initial Configuration Tasks window, click *Configure networking*. The Network Connections window appears.

3. Right-click the *Local Area Connection* icon and, from the context menu, select Properties. The Local Area Connection Properties sheet appears.

4. Select Internet Protocol Version 4 (TCP/IPv4) and click *Properties*. The Internet Protocol Version 4 (TCP/IPv4) Properties sheet appears.

5. In the IP address text box, type **10.0.0.*xx***, where *xx* is the number your instructor assigned to your server.

6. In the Subnet mask text box, type **255.255.255.0**.

7. In the Default gateway text box, type **10.0.0.1.**

8. Leave the Preferred DNS server text box set to 127.0.0.1.

9. Click *OK* to close the Internet Protocol Version 4 (TCP/IPv4) Properties sheet.

10. Click *OK* to close the Local Area Connection Properties sheet.

11. Close the Network Connections window.

12. Leave the server logged on for the next exercise.

Exercise 8.2	Installing the Remote Desktop Services Role
Overview	For Windows Server 2008 R2 to function as a Remote Desktop Services server, you must first install the Remote Desktop Services role. Add the role with the role services that enable the server to provide three types of Remote Desktop functionality.
Completion time	15 minutes

1. Click *Start*. Then click *Administrative tools > Server Manager*. The Server Manager Console appears.

2. Select the Roles node and click *Add Roles*. The Add Roles Wizard appears.

3.   Click *Next* to bypass the *Before You Begin* page. The *Select Server Roles* page appears.

4.   Select the Remote Desktop Services check box and click *Next*. The *Remote Desktop Services* page appears.

5.   Click *Next* to continue. The *Select Role Services* page appears, as shown in Figure 8-1.

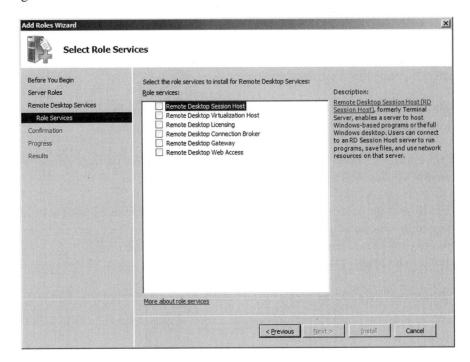

Figure 8-1
The *Select Role Services* page of the Add Roles Wizard

6.   Select the Remote Desktop Session Host check box. An Add Roles Wizard message box appears, warning you of the security hazard of installing Remote Desktop Services on a domain controller.

7.   Click *Install Remote Desktop Session Host* anyway (not recommended).

> **NOTE**   *In a laboratory environment, it is safe to install Remote Desktop Services along with Active Directory Domain Services. However, this is not a safe practice in a production environment.*

8.   Select the Remote Desktop Web Access check box. The Add role services and features required for Remote Desktop Web Access? dialog box appears.

9.   Click *Add Required Role Services*.

10. Click *Next*. The *Uninstall and Reinstall Applications for Compatibility* page appears.

11. Click *Next*. The *Specify Authentication Method for Terminal Server* page appears.

12. Select the Do Not Require Network Level Authentication option and click *Next*. The *Specify Licensing Mode* page appears.

13. Select the Configure Later option and click *Next*. The *Select User Groups Allowed to Access This RD Session Host Server* page appears.

14. Click *Next*. The *Configure Client Experience* page appears.

15. Click *Next* to accept the default settings. The *Web Server (IIS)* page appears.

16. Click *Next*. The *Select Role Services* page appears.

17. Click *Next* to accept the default selections. The *Confirm Installation Selections* page appears.

18. Take a screen shot of the *Confirm Installation Selections* page by pressing Ctrl+Prt Scr, and then paste the resulting image into the Lab08_worksheet file in the page provided by pressing Ctrl+V.

19. Click *Install*. The wizard installs the role and the *Installation Results* page appears.

20. Click *Close*. An Add Roles Wizard message box appears, prompting you to restart the computer.

21. Click *Yes*. The computer restarts.

22. When the logon screen appears, log on using your **Administrator** account and the password **Pa$$w0rd.** Server Manager loads, and completes the role installation.

23. Click *Close*.

24. Close Server Manager and leave the computer logged on for the next exercise.

Exercise 8.3	Configuring RemoteApp Applications
Overview	Configure your Remote Desktop server to deploy individual applications using RemoteApp.
Completion time	10 minutes

1. Click *Start*. Then click *Administrative Tools > Remote Desktop Services > RemoteApp Manager*. The RemoteApp Manager console appears, as shown in Figure 8-2.

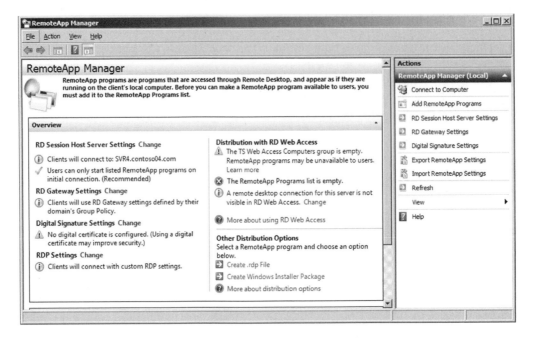

Figure 8-2
The RemoteApp Manager console

2. In the actions pane, click *Add RemoteAppPrograms*. The RemoteApp Wizard appears.

3. Click *Next* to bypass the *Welcome* page. The *Choose Programs To Add To The RemoteApp Programs List* page appears.

4. Select the WordPad check box and click *Properties*. The RemoteApp Properties sheet for WordPad appears.

5. Select the RemoteApp Program Is Available Through RD Web Access check box.

6. Select the Allow any command-line arguments option and click *OK*. A RemoteApp Wizard message box appears, warning you that allowing executable files to run with no restrictions on the command line arguments opens the RD Session Host server to attack.

7. Click *Yes*.

8. Click *Next*. The *Review Settings* page appears.

9. Click *Finish*. The WordPad application appears in the RemoteApp Programs list.

10. Using the same procedure, add the Calculator and System Information applications to the RemoteApp Programs list, clearing the RemoteApp program is available through RD Web Access check box and leaving the default Do not allow command-line arguments setting for each.

11. Take a screen shot of the RemoteApp Manager console, showing the applications you added. by pressing Ctrl+Prt Scr, and then paste the resulting image into the Lab08_worksheet file in the page provided by pressing Ctrl+V.

Question 1	*In the RemoteApp Manager console, there are currently two warning indicators showing in the Overview area. Will either of these warnings make it impossible to access your RemoteApp applications from your partner server? Explain why or why not.*

12. Close the RemoteApp Manager console.

13. Leave the computer logged on for the next exercise.

Exercise 8.4	Creating an RDP File
Overview	Use the Remote Desktop Connection client to create an RDP file that you can deploy to other computers, enabling them to connect to your Remote Desktop server using a predetermined collection of configuration settings.
Completion time	10 minutes

1. Click *Start*. Then click *All Programs > Accessories > Remote Desktop Connection*. The Remote Desktop Connection dialog box appears.

2. Click *Options*. The dialog box expands, as shown in Figure 8-3.

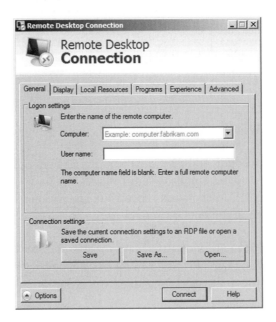

Figure 8-3
The Remote Desktop Connection dialog box

3. In the Computer text box, type **10.0.0.xx**, where *xx* is the number your instructor assigned to your server.

Question 2	Why is it necessary, in this particular case, to use the server's IP address in the Computer text box, rather than its name?

4. In the User name text box, type **Administrator.**

5. Click the *Display* tab.

6. In the Remote Desktop Size box, set the slider to 640 by 480 pixels.

7. Click the *General* tab.

8. In the Connection Settings box, click *Save As*. The Save As combo box appears.

9. Select the Favorites\Downloads folder.

10. In the File Name text box, type **SVRxx,** where *xx* is the number your instructor assigned to your server.

11. Click *Save*. The program saves the SVRxx.rdp file to the Downloads folder.

12. Leave the computer logged in for the next exercise.

Exercise 8.5	Creating RemoteApp RDP Files
Overview	Create RDP files that enable clients to access the RemoteApp applications you configured in Exercise 8.3.
Completion time	10 minutes

1. Click *Start*. Then click *Administrative Tools > Remote Desktop Services > RemoteApp Manager*. The RemoteApp Manager console appears.

2. In the RemoteApp Programs list, select the WordPad application you added in Exercise 8.3.

3. In the actions pane, select Create .rdp File. The RemoteApp Wizard appears.

4. Click *Next* to bypass the *Welcome to the RemoteApp Wizard* page. The *Specify Package Settings* page appears, as shown in Figure 8-4.

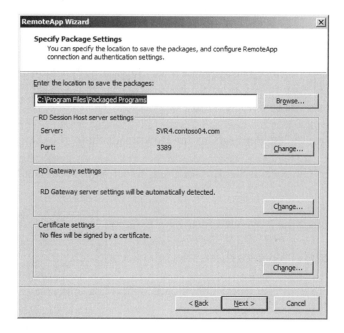

Figure 8-4
The *Specify Package Settings* page of the RemoteApp
Wizard

5. Click *Browse*. The Browse for folder dialog box appears.

6. Browse to the C:\Users\Administrator\Downloads folder and click *OK*. The path to the folder appears in the Enter the location to save the packages text box.

7. Click *Next*. The *Review Settings* page appears.

8. Click *Finish*. The wizard closes and the wizard creates an RDP file named for the application in the Documents folder.

9. Repeat the process to create an RDP file for the Calculator application in the Documents folder.

10. Close the RemoteApp Manager console.

Exercise 8.6	Creating a Share
Overview	Share the Downloads folder in which you saved your RDP file, so that your partner can access it from his or her server.
Completion time	10 minutes

1. Click *Start*. Then click *All Programs > Accessories > Windows Explorer*. The Windows Explorer window appears.

2. Browse to the C:\Users\Administrator\Downloads folder.

3. Right-click the *Downloads* folder and, from the context menu, select Properties. The Downloads Properties sheet appears.

4. Click the *Sharing* tab.

5. Click *Advanced Sharing*. The Advanced Sharing dialog box appears.

6. Select the Share this folder check box.

7. Click *Permissions*. The Permissions for Downloads dialog box appears.

8. With the Everyone special identity selected, select Allow Full Control and click *OK*.

9. Click *OK* to close the Advanced Sharing dialog box.

10. In the Downloads Properties sheet, select the Security tab.

11. Click *Edit*. The Permissions for Downloads dialog box appears.

12. Click *Add*. The Select Users, Computers, Service Accounts, or Groups dialog box appears.

13. In the Enter the object names to select box, type **Everyone** and click *OK*. The Everyone special identity appears in the Group or user names list.

14. Wth the Everyone special identity selected, select the Allow Modify check box and click *OK*.

15. Click *Close* to close the Downloads Properties dialog box.

16. Leave the computer logged in for the next exercise.

Exercise 8.7	Using the Remote Desktop Connection Client
Overview	Connect to Remote Desktop Services on your partner's server, using the Remote Desktop Connection client.
Completion time	10 minutes

> **NOTE**
>
> *It will be necessary for you and your lab partner to take turns connecting to each other's servers, because it is not possible for the two computers to establish RD connections to each other simultaneously.*

1. Click *Start*. Then click *All Programs > Accessories > Remote Desktop Connection*. The Remote Desktop Connection dialog box appears.

2. Click *Options*. The dialog box expands.

3. Click the *Display* tab.

4. In the Remote Desktop Size box, set the slider to 640 by 480 pixels.

5. Click the *Local Resources* tab.

6. In the Remote audio box, select Settings. A Remote Desktop Connection dialog box appears.

7. In the Remote audio playback box, select the Do not play option and click *OK*.

8. In the Local Devices and Resources box, clear the Printers check box and leave the Clipboard check box selected.

9. Click the *Experience* tab.

10. In the Choose your connection speed to optimize performance drop-down list, select LAN (10 Mbps Or Higher).

11. Click the *General* tab.

12. In the Computer text box, type **10.0.0.**xx, where *xx* is the number your instructor assigned to your partner's server.

13. In the User Name field, type **contoso**xx**Administrator,** where xx is the number your instructor assigned to your partner's server.

Question 3	Why would it not be possible to connect to your partner's server using the Administrator account from your domain?

NOTE	Before you initiate the connection to your partner server, make sure that Exercise 8.1 has been completed on that computer, and that it is ready to receive remote connections.

14. Click *Connect*. A Windows Security dialog box appears.

15. Under the contosoxx\\Administrator user name, type **Pa$$w0rd** and click *OK*. A Remote Desktop Connection message box appears, warning you of a certificate problem.

16. Click *Yes*. A 10.0.0.xx – Remote Desktop Connection window appears containing the desktop of your partner server.

17. In the 10.0.0.xx - Remote Desktop Connection window, click *Start*. Then click *All Programs > Accessories > Notepad*. A Notepad window appears.

18. Take a screen shot of the 10.0.0.xx – Remote Desktop Connection window by pressing Ctrl+Prt Scr, and then paste the resulting image into the Lab08_worksheet file in the page provided by pressing Ctrl+V.

Question 4	On which computer is the Notepad application actually running?

19. Leave the Notepad window open and click the *Close* button in the title bar of the 10.0.0.xx - Remote Desktop Connection window. A Remote Desktop Connection message box appears, asking if you want to disconnect.

20. Click *OK*. The RDC client disconnects from the Remote Desktop server.

Question 5	Is Notepad still running on your partner's server? Explain why or why not.

21. Leave the computer logged on for the next exercise.

Exercise 8.8	Connecting Using RDP Files
Overview	Connect to Remote Desktop Services on your partner server, using the RDP files you created earlier.
Completion time	10 minutes

1. Click *Start*. Then click *Run*. The Run dialog box appears.

2. In the open text box, type **10.0.0.*xx*\Downloads** and click *OK*. A Windows Explorer window appears, displaying the contents of the Downloads folder.

3. Double-click the *SVRxx.rdp file*. A Remote Desktop Connection window appears, warning you that the publisher of the RDP file could not be identified.

4. Click *Connect*. A Windows Security dialog box appears.

5. Under the Administrator user name, type **Pa$$w0rd** and click *OK*. A Remote Desktop Connection message box appears, warning you of a certificate problem.

6. Click *Yes*. An SVRxx - 10.0.0.xx – Remote Desktop Connection window appears, containing the desktop of your partner's server.

Question 6	How can you tell that you are connected to the same server as in Exercise 8.7?

7. Close the SVRxx - 10.0.0.xx – Remote Desktop Connection window, disconnecting you from your partner's server.

8. In Windows Explorer, double-click the *WordPad.rdp file*. A RemoteApp message box appears, warning you that the publisher of the RDP file could not be identified.

9. Click *Connect*. A Windows Security dialog box appears.

10. Under the contoso*xx*\Administrator user name, type **Pa$$w0rd** and click *OK*. A Document – WordPad window appears.

Question 7	On which computer is the Wordpad.exe file running?

11. Take a screen shot of the Document – WordPad window by pressing Ctrl+Prt Scr, and then paste the resulting image into the Lab08_worksheet file in the page provided by pressing Ctrl+V.

12. Click the *WordPad icon,* and then click *Open.* The open combo box appears.

13. Browse to the Favorites\Downloads folder.

Question 8	*Are you looking at the Downloads folder on your computer or on your partner's server, the Remote Desktop server? How can you tell?*

14. Click *Cancel* to close the Open combo box.

15. Close the Document – WordPad window.

16. Leave the computer logged on for the next exercise.

Exercise 8.9	Connecting Using RD Web Access
Overview	Connect to Remote Desktop Services on your partner's server, using the RD Web Access interface you installed in Exercise 8.2.
Completion time	10 minutes

1. Click *Start.* Then click *Administrative Tools > Server Manager.* The Server Manager window appears.

2. Click the *Configure IE ESC link.* The Internet Explorer Enhanced Security Configuration dialog box appears.

3. Under Administrators, select Off and click *OK.*

4. Close the Server Manager window.

5. Click *Start.* Then click *Internet Explorer.* The Internet Explorer window appears.

6. In the address box, type **http://10.0.0.xx/rdweb** and press Enter. *A Certificate Error: Navigation Blocked* page appears.

7. Click *Continue* to this Web site (not recommended). The RD Web Access page appears.

8. Click the yellow *Information Bar* and, from the context menu, select Run Add-on. An Internet Explorer – Security Warning message box appears, warning you of the ActiveX code in the add-on.

9. Click *Run*. The *Remote Desktop Services Default Connection* page appears, as shown in Figure 8-5.

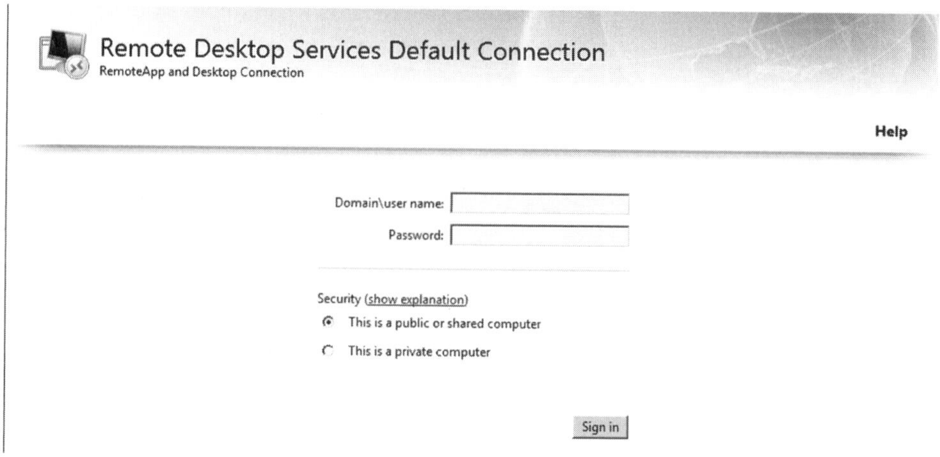

Figure 8-5
The *Remote Desktop Services Default Connection* page

10. In the Domain\user name and Password text boxes, type credentials for your partner's server and click *Sign in*. A new page appears, containing the WordPad RemoteApp program you designated as Web deployable.

11. Double-click the *WordPad icon*. A RemoteApp message box appears.

12. Click *Connect*. A Windows Security dialog box appears.

13. Type in your credentials for the RemoteApp program, and click *Connect*. A RemoteApp message box appears, warning you of a certificate problem.

14. Click *Yes*. The WordPad window appears.

15. Close the Wordpad window.

16. Leave the computer logged on for the next exercise.

Exercise 8.10	Restoring TCP/IP Settings
Overview	Once you have completed your work with Remote Desktop Services, you can return your server to its original TCP/IP configuration.
Completion time	5 minutes

1. In the Initial Configuration Tasks window, click *Configure networking*. The Network Connections window appears.

2. Right-click the *Local Area Connection* icon and, from the context menu, select *Properties*. The Local Area Connection Properties sheet appears.

3.   Select Internet Protocol Version 4 (TCP/IPv4) and click *Properties*. The Internet Protocol Version 4 (TCP/IPv4) Properties sheet appears.

4.   In the IP address text box, type **10.0.*xx*.1**, where *xx* is the number your instructor assigned to your server.

5.   In the Subnet mask text box, type **255.255.255.0**.

6.   In the Default gateway text box, remove the current setting and leave the box blank.

7.   Leave the Preferred DNS server text box set to **127.0.0.1**.

8.   Click *OK* to close the Internet Protocol Version 4 (TCP/IPv4) Properties sheet.

9.   Click *OK* to close the Local Area Connection Properties sheet.

10. Close the Network Connections window.

11. Log off of the server.

LAB 9
DEPLOYING UPDATES

This lab contains the following exercises and activities:

Exercise 9.1   Reconfiguring TCP/IP

Exercise 9.2   Installing the WSUS Role

Exercise 9.3   Configuring WSUS

Exercise 9.4   Using the Update Services Console

Exercise 9.5   Configuring Windows Updates

Exercise 9.6   Restoring TCP/IP Settings

BEFORE YOU BEGIN

The lab environment consists of student servers connected to a local area network, along with a classroom server that functions as the domain controller for a domain called contoso.com. Each student has his or her own server, which functions as a domain controller for a separate forest. Most of the exercises in this manual will require each student to work on his or her own domain controller in a separate Active Directory Domain Services domain.

> **NOTE**
>
> *In the classroom lab environment, the instructor originally assigned each server a number that the student used to form the server's IP address, computer name, and domain name, as specified in Lab 1. This kept each server in its own separate environment and prevented server interaction. For this lab, however, interaction between servers in different forests is needed, so you will begin by reconfiguring your server's TCP/IP settings, to place your server on a common classroom subnet. You must complete Exercise 9.1 before you proceed to the other exercises.*

In addition to the computers, you will also require the software listed in Table 9-1 to complete Lab 9.

Table 9-1
Software required for Lab 9

Software	Location
Lab 9 student worksheet	Lab09_worksheet.rtf (provided by instructor)

Working with Lab Worksheets

Each lab in this manual requires that you answer questions, shoot screen shots, and perform other activities that you will document in a worksheet named for the lab, such as Lab09_worksheet.rtf. Your instructor will provide you with access to the worksheets. It is recommended that you use a USB flash drive to store your worksheets, so you can submit them to your instructor for review. As you perform the exercises in each lab, open the appropriate worksheet file using WordPad, fill in the required information, and save the file to your flash drive.

SCENARIO

You are an enterprise administrator working in a lab environment where you are testing designs for the Windows Server 2008 R2 infrastructure services that your company will need for a new division it is deploying in the near future. In your current lab scenario, you are evaluating the capabilities of Windows Server Update Services.

After completing this lab, you will be able to:

■ Install a WSUS Server

■ Configure a Synchronization Strategy

■ Approve Updates

■ Configure Windows Update clients using Group Policy

Estimated lab time: 75 minutes

Exercise 9.1	Reconfiguring TCP/IP
Overview	To accommodate the installation of WSUS, you must modify your server's IP address so that you can access the Internet.
Completion time	5 minutes

1. Log on to your server using the **Administrator** account and the password **Pa$$w0rd**. The Initial Configuration Tasks window appears.

2. In the Initial Configuration Tasks window, click *Configure networking*. The Network Connections window appears.

3. Right-click the *Local Area Connection* icon and, from the context menu, select *Properties*. The Local Area Connection Properties sheet appears.

4. Select Internet Protocol Version 4 (TCP/IPv4) and click *Properties*. The Internet Protocol Version 4 (TCP/IPv4) Properties sheet appears.

5. In the IP address text box, type **10.0.0.xx**, where *xx* is the number your instructor assigned to your server.

6. In the Subnet mask text box, type **255.255.255.0**.

7. In the Default gateway text box, type **10.0.0.1.**

8. Leave the Preferred DNS server text box set to 127.0.0.1.

9. Click *OK* to close the Internet Protocol Version 4 (TCP/IPv4) Properties sheet.

10. Click *OK* to close the Local Area Connection Properties sheet.

11. Close the Network Connections window.

12. Leave the server logged on for the next exercise.

Exercise 9.2	Installing the WSUS Role
Overview	Install the Windows Server Update Services role.
Completion time	10 minutes

1. Click *Start*. Then click *Administrative Tools > Server Manager*. The Server Manager console appears.

2. Select the Roles node and, in the detail pane, click *Add Roles*. The Add Roles Wizard appears.

3. Click *Next* to bypass the *Before You Begin* page. The *Select Server Roles* page appears, as shown in Figure 9-1.

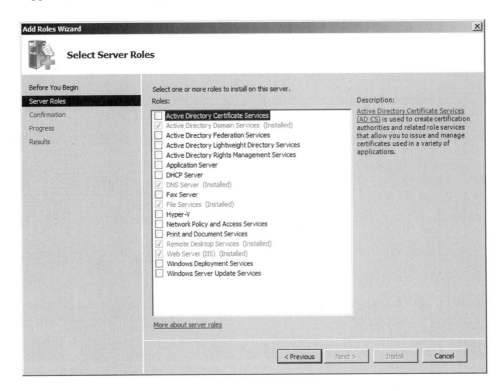

Figure 9-1
The *Select Server Roles* page of the Add Roles Wizard

4. Select the Windows Server Update Services check box. The Add role services required for Windows Server Update Services? dialog box appears.

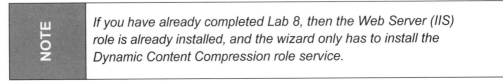

> **NOTE** *If you have already completed Lab 8, then the Web Server (IIS) role is already installed, and the wizard only has to install the Dynamic Content Compression role service.*

5. Click *Add Required Role Services*. Then click *Next*. The *Web Server (IIS)* page appears.

6. Click *Next*. The *Select Role Services* page appears.

7. Click *Next*. The *Windows Server Update Services* page appears.

8. Click *Next*. The *Confirm Installation Selections* page appears.

9. Click *Install*. The *Installation Progress* page appears as the wizard installs the role. The Windows Server Update Services 3.0 SP2 Setup Wizard appears.

10. Click *Next* to bypass the *Welcome* page. *The License Agreement* page appears.

11. Select the I accept the terms of the license agreement option and click *Next*. The *Required Components to use administration UI* page appears. Click *Next*. The *Select Update Source* page appears.

12. Leave the Store updates locally check box selected and click *Next* to accept the default path. The *Database Options* page appears.

13. Click *Next* to accept the default settings. The *Web Site Selection* page appears.

14. Leave the Use the existing IIS Default Web site option selected and click *Next*. The *Ready to Install Windows Server Update Services 3.0 SP2* page appears.

15. Click *Next*. The *Installing* page appears, as the wizard installs WSUS. The *Completing the Windows Server Update Services 3.0 SP2 Setup Wizard* page appears.

16. Click *Finish*. The Wizard completes the process and the *Installation Results* page appears.

17. Click *Close*. The Windows Server Update Services Configuration Wizard appears.

18. Leave the wizard open for the next exercise.

Exercise 9.3	Configuring WSUS
Overview	Configure Windows Server Update Services.
Completion time	15 minutes

1. In the Windows Server Update Services Configuration Wizard, click *Next* to bypass the *Before You Begin* page. The *Join the Microsoft Update Improvement Program* page appears.

2. Clear the Yes, I would like to join the Microsoft Update Improvement Program check box and click *Next. The Choose Upstream Server* page appears, as shown in Figure 9-2.

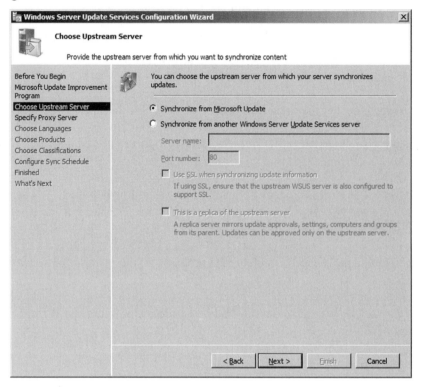

Figure 9-2
The *Choose Upstream Server* page of the Windows Server Update Services Configuration Wizard

3. Click *Next* to accept the default setting. The *Specify Proxy Server* page appears.

> **NOTE** *If your classroom network does not have access to the Internet, your instructor will supply you with alternative settings for this page that will enable your server to download updates from another server in the classroom.*

4. Click *Next* to accept the default settings. The *Connect to Upstream Server* page appears.

5. Click *Start Connecting.* The wizard establishes a connection to the upstream server, which can take several minutes.

6. Click *Next.* The *Choose Languages* page appears.

7. Click *Next* to accept the default settings. The *Choose Products* page appears.

8. Click *Next* to accept the default settings. The *Choose Classifications* page appears.

9. Select the Update Rollups and Updates check boxes and click *Next*. The *Set Sync Schedule* page appears.

10. Click *Next* to accept the default settings. The *Finished* page appears.

11. Take a screen shot of the *Finished* page, by pressing Ctrl+Prt Scr, and then paste the resulting image into the lab09_worksheet file in the page provided by pressing Ctrl+V.

12. Clear the Begin initial synchronization check box and click *Next*. The *What's Next* page appears.

13. Click *Finish*. The wizard closes.

14. Leave the server logged on for the next exercise.

Exercise 9.4	Using the Update Services Console
Overview	Synchronize the WSUS server and approve an update for deployment.
Completion time	30 minutes

1. Click *Start*. Then click *Administrative Tools > Windows Server Update Services*. The Update Services console appears.

2. In the scope (left) pane, select the SVRxx node, as shown in Figure 9-3.

Figure 9-3
The Update Services console

3. In the detail pane, click *Synchronize now*.

4. Wait for the synchronization process to finish. This could take some time, depending on the speed of your connection.

Question 1	*How many critical and security updates did WSUS download?*

5. Take a screen shot of the Update Services console by pressing Ctrl+Prt Scr and then paste the resulting image into the Lab09_worksheet file in the page provided by pressing Ctrl+V.

6. In the scope pane, expand the SVRxx and Computers nodes.

7. Right-click *All Computers* and, from the context menu, select Add Computer Group. The Add Computer Group dialog box appears.

8. In the Name text box, type **Servers** and click *Add*. The new group appears under the All Computers node.

NOTE	*Please note that groups you create in the Update Services console are not in any way related to Active Directory groups or the computer's local groups.*

9. In the scope pane, select Options.

10. In the detail pane, select Computers. The Computers dialog box appears.

11. Select Use Group Policy or registry settings on computers and click *OK*.

12. In the scope pane, expand the Updates node. Then select All Updates.

13. In the detail pane, in the Status drop-down list, select Any. A list of the downloaded updates appears in the detail pane.

14. Click the *Classification column head* to resort the list.

15. Scroll down in the list of updates and select the first Windows Server 2008 entry for your processing platform.

16. In the actions pane, click *Approve*. The Approve Updates dialog box appears.

17. Select the Servers group, click the *down arrow* and, from the context menu, select Approved for Install. Then click *OK*. An Approval Progress dialog box appears.

Question 2	*What was the result of the approval process?*

18. Click *Close*.

19. Take a screen shot of the Update Services console, showing the list of updates, by pressing Ctrl+Prt Scr and then paste the resulting image into the Lab09_worksheet file in the page provided by pressing Ctrl+V.

20. Close the Update Services console.

21. Leave the server logged on for the next exercise.

Exercise 9.5	Configuring Windows Updates
Overview	In this exercise, you create a Group Policy object that configures the Windows Updates policies for the servers on your network.
Completion time	10 minutes

1. Click *Start*. Then click *Administrative Tools > Group Policy Management*. The Group Policy Management console appears.

2. Browse to the contoso*xx*.com domain, where *xx* is the number your instructor assigned to your server.

3. Right-click the *Group Policy Objects* container and, from the context menu, select New. The New GPO dialog box appears.

4. In the Name text box, type **Server Updates** and click *OK*. The new GPO appears in the Group Policy Objects container.

5. Right-click the GPO you just created and, from the context menu, select Edit. The Group Policy Management Editor console appears.

6. Browse to the Computer Configuration\Policies\Administrative Templates\Windows Components container, as shown in Figure 9-4.

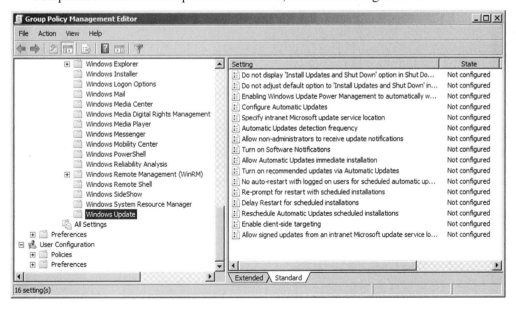

Figure 9-4
The Windows Components container

7.   Double-click the *Configure Automatic Updates* policy. The Configure Automatic Updates dialog box appears.

8.   Select the Enabled option.

9.   In the Configure automatic updating drop-down list, select 4 – Auto download and schedule the install.

10. In the Scheduled install day drop-down list, select 1 – Every Sunday.

11. In the Scheduled install time drop-down list, select 05:00.

12. Take a screen shot of the Configure Automatic Updates dialog box by pressing Ctrl+Prt Scr and then paste the resulting image into the Lab09_worksheet file in the page provided by pressing Ctrl+V.

13. Click *OK*.

14. Double-click the *Specify intranet Micrsoft update service location policy*. The Specify intranet Micrsoft update service location policy dialog box appears.

15. Select the Enabled option.

16. In the Set the intranet update service for detecting updates text box, type **http://svr*xx***, where *xx* is the number your instructor assigned to your server.

17. In the Set the intranet statistics server text box, type **http://svr*xx***, where *xx* is the number your instructor assigned to your server. Then click *OK*.

18. Double-click the *Enable client-side targeting* policy. The Enable client-side targeting Properties dialog box appears.

19. Select the Enabled option.

20. In the Target group name for this computer text box, type **Servers** and click *OK*.

21. Close the Group Policy Management Editor console.

Exercise 9.6	Restoring TCP/IP Settings
Overview	Once you have completed your work with Windows Server Update Services, you can return your server to its original TCP/IP configuration.
Completion time	5 minutes

1.   In the *Initial Configuration Tasks* window, click *Configure networking*. The Network Connections window appears.

2.   Right-click the *Local Area Connection* icon and, from the context menu, select *Properties*. The Local Area Connection Properties sheet appears.

3.   Select Internet Protocol Version 4 (TCP/IPv4) and click *Properties*. The Internet Protocol Version 4 (TCP/IPv4) Properties sheet appears.

4.   In the IP address text box, type **10.0.*xx*.1**, where *xx* is the number your instructor assigned to your server.

5.   In the Subnet mask text box, type **255.255.255.0**.

6.   In the Default gateway text box, remove the current setting and leave the box blank.

7.   Leave the Preferred DNS server text box set to 127.0.0.1.

8.   Click *OK* to close the Internet Protocol Version 4 (TCP/IPv4) Properties sheet.

9.   Click *OK* to close the Local Area Connection Properties sheet.

10. Close the Network Connections window.

11. Log off of the server.

LAB 10
CONFIGURING NETWORK ACCESS

This lab contains the following exercises and activities:

BEFORE YOU BEGIN

The lab environment consists of student servers connected to a local area network, along with a classroom server that functions as the domain controller for a domain called contoso.com. Each student has his or her own server, which functions as a domain controller for a separate forest. Most of the exercises in this manual will require each student to work on his or her own domain controller in a separate Active Directory Domain Services domain.

> NOTE
>
> *In the classroom lab environment, the instructor originally assigned each server a number that the student used to form the server's IP address, computer name, and domain name, as specified in Lab 1. This kept each server in its own separate environment and prevented server interaction. For this lab, however, interaction between servers in different forests is needed, so you will begin by reconfiguring your server's TCP/IP settings, to place your server on a common classroom subnet. You must complete Exercise 10.1 before you proceed to the other exercises.*

In addition to the computers, you will also require the software listed in Table 10-1 to complete Lab 10.

Table 10-1
Software required for Lab 10

Software	Location
Lab 10 student worksheet	Lab10_worksheet.rtf (provided by instructor)

Working with Lab Worksheets

Each lab in this manual requires that you answer questions, shoot screen shots, and perform other activities that you will document in a worksheet named for the lab, such as Lab09_worksheet.rtf. Your instructor will provide you with access to the worksheets. It is recommended that you use a USB flash drive to store your worksheets, so you can submit them to your instructor for review. As you perform the exercises in each lab, open the appropriate worksheet file using WordPad, fill in the required information, and save the file to your flash drive.

SCENARIO

You are an enterprise administrator working in a lab environment where you are testing remote access strategies that your company will need for a new division it is deploying in the near future. In your current lab scenario, you are evaluating the VPN server capabilities of Windows Server 2008 R2.

> NOTE
>
> *Before you begin this lab exercise, select another student in the classroom to function as your partner. You will use each other's servers to establish VPN connections.*

After completing this lab, you will be able to:

- Install the Network Policy and Access Services role

- Configure RRAS

- Configure the VPN client

- Extablish a VPN connection

Estimated lab time: 50 minutes

Exercise 10.1	Reconfiguring TCP/IP
Overview	To accommodate the installation of RRAS, you must modify your server's IP address, so that you can access your partner's server on the classroom network.
Completion time	5 minutes

1. Log on to your server using the **Administrator** account and the password **Pa$$w0rd**. The Initial Configuration Tasks window appears.

2. In the Initial Configuration Tasks window, click *Configure networking*. The Network Connections window appears.

3. Right-click the *Local Area Connection icon* and, from the context menu, select Properties. The Local Area Connection Properties sheet appears.

4. Select Internet Protocol Version 4 (TCP/IPv4) and click *Properties*. The Internet Protocol Version 4 (TCP/IPv4) Properties sheet appears.

5. In the IP address text box, type **10.0.0.xx**, where *xx* is the number your instructor assigned to your server.

6. In the Subnet mask text box, type **255.255.255.0**.

7. In the Default gateway text box, type **10.0.0.1.**

8. Leave the Preferred DNS server text box set to 127.0.0.1.

9. Click *OK* to close the Internet Protocol Version 4 (TCP/IPv4) Properties sheet.

10. Click *OK* to close the Local Area Connection Properties sheet.

11. Close the Network Connections window.

12. Leave the server logged on for the next exercise.

Exercise 10.2	Installing Network Policy and Access Services
Overview	Install the Network Policy and Access Services role, which includes the Routing and Remote Access Service. RRAS enables the server to receive VPN connections from clients on the Internet.
Completion time	5 minutes

1. Click *Start*. Then click *Administrative Tools > Server Manager*. The Server Manager console appears.

2. Select the Roles node and click *Add Roles*. The Add Roles Wizard appears, displaying the *Before You Begin* page.

3. Click *Next* to continue. The *Select Server Roles* page appears.

4. Select the Network Policy and Access Services role and click *Next*. The *Introduction to Network Policy and Access Services* page appears.

5. Click *Next* to continue. The *Select Role Services* page appears, as shown in Figure 10-1.

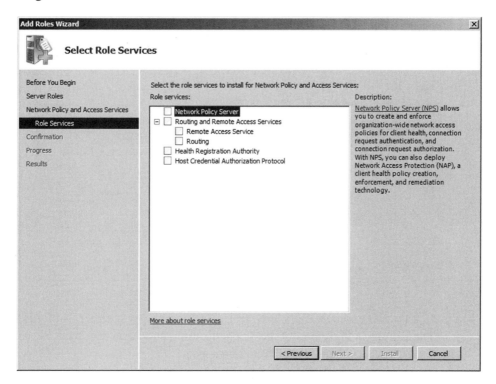

Figure 10-1
The *Select Role Services* page of the Add Roles Wizard

6. Select the Remote Access Service check box and click *Next*. The *Confirm Installation Selections* page appears.

7. Click *Install*. The wizard installs the role and the *Installation Results* page appears.

8. Click *Close*. The wizard closes.

9. Close the Server Manager console.

10. Leave the computer logged on for the next exercise.

Exercise 10.3	Configuring Routing and Remote Access
Overview	Routing and Remote Access can perform a variety of services. Configure the service to function as a VPN server.
Completion time	10 minutes

1. Click *Start*. Then click *Administrative Tools > Routing and Remote Access*. The Routing and Remote Access console appears, as shown in Figure 10-2.

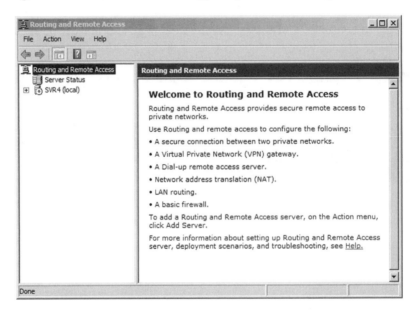

Figure 10-2
The Routing and Remote Access console

2. Right-click the *SVRxx* (local) node and, from the context menu, select Configure and Enable Routing and Remote Access. The Routing and Remote Access Server Setup Wizard appears, displaying the *Welcome* page.

3. Click *Next*. The *Configuration* page appears.

4. Select the Custom Configuration option and click *Next*. The *Custom Configuration* page appears.

5. Select the VPN access check box and click *Next*. The *Completing the Routing and Remote Access Server Setup Wizard* page appears.

6. Click *Finish*. A Routing and Remote Access message box appears, informing you that the service is ready to start.

7. Click *Start service*. The wizard configures the service and closes.

8. Take a screen shot of the Routing and Remote Access console by pressing Ctrl+Prt Scr and then paste the resulting image into the Lab10_worksheet file in the page provided by pressing Ctrl+V.

9. Leave the Routing and Remote Access console open for the next exercise.

Exercise 10.4	Configuring a VPN Client
Overview	At this point, your server is configured to function as a VPN server. Configure Windows Server 2008 R2 to function as a VPN client, so you can establish a connection to your partner's server.
Completion time	10 minutes

1. Click *Start*, and then click *Control Panel*. The Control Panel window appears.

2. Click *Network and Internet*. Then click *Network and Sharing Center*. The Network and Sharing Center window appears.

3. Click *Set up a new connection or network*. The Set up a connection or network wizard appears, displaying the *Choose a connection option* page, as shown in Figure 10-3.

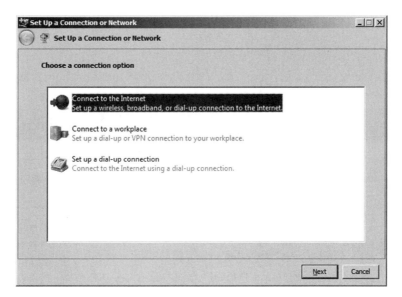

Figure 10-3
The *Choose a connection option* page of the Set up a connection or network wizard

4. Select *Connect to a workplace* and click *Next*. The *How do you want to connect?* page appears.

5. Click *Use my Internet connection (VPN)*. The *Do you want to set up an Internet connection before continuing?* page appears.

6. Click *I'll set up an Internet connection later*. The *Type the Internet address to connect to* page appears.

7. In the *Internet address* text box, type **10.0.0.xx**, where *xx* is the number your instructor assigned to your partner's server.

8. In the *Destination name* text box, type **SVRxx VPN Connection**.

9. Select the Allow other people to use this connection check box, and click *Next*. The *Type your user name and password* page appears.

10. In the User name text box, type **Administrator**.

11. In the Password text box, type **Pa$$w0rd**.

12. Click *Create*. A *The connection is ready to use* page appears.

13. Click *Close*. The wizard closes.

14. In the Network and Sharing Center, click *Connect to a Network*. An untitled window appears, containing a list of the computer's connections, with the SVR*xx* VPN Connection you created among them.

15. Take a screen shot of the window by pressing Ctrl+Prt Scr and then paste the resulting image into the Lab10_worksheet file in the page provided by pressing Ctrl+V.

16. Leave the Network and Sharing Center window open for the next exercise.

Exercise 10.5	Establishing a Connection
Overview	Use the client on your server to establish a VPN connection with your partner server.
Completion time	15 minutes

NOTE	*Before you begin this exercise, make sure that your lab partner has completed Exercises 10.1 to 10.4 on his or her server. Also, you and your partner must take turns using your VPN clients to establish connections to each other's servers. Connecting each client to the other server simultaneously can result in unstable connections.*

1.   In the Network and Sharing Center, click *Connect to a network*. The window listing the available connections appears.

2.   Select SVRxx VPN Connection and click *Connect*. The Connect SVRxx VPN Connection dialog box appears, as shown in Figure 10-4.

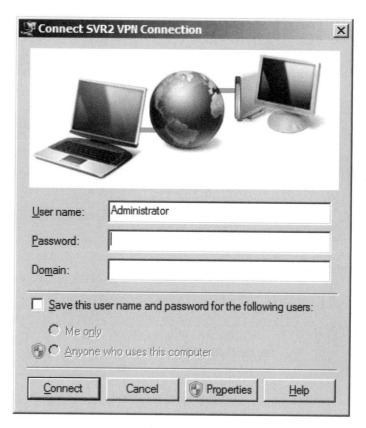

Figure 10-4
The Connect SVRxx VPN Connection dialog box

3.   In the Password text box, type **Pa$$w0rd** and click *Connect*.

Question 1	*What happens?*

4.   Take a screen shot of the window displaying the results of the connection attempt by pressing Ctrl+Prt Scr and then paste the resulting image into the Lab10_worksheet file in the page provided by pressing Ctrl+V.

5.   Click *Close*.

6.   Click *Start*. Then click *Administrative Tools > Active Directory Users and Computers*. The Active Directory Users and Computers console appears.

7. Expand the contoso.com node and select the Users container.

8. Double-click the *Administrator* user object. The Administrator Properties sheet appears.

9. Click the *Dial-in* tab.

10. In the Network Access Permission box, select Allow Access and click *OK*.

11. Close the Active Directory Users and Computers console.

NOTE	*Make sure that your lab partner has completed steps 5 to 9 before you proceed.*

12. Repeat steps 1 to 3 to try connecting to your partner server again, using the following credentials:

   - User name: **Administrator**

   - Password: **Pa$$w0rd**

Question 2	*What happens this time?*

13. When your partner server successfully connects to your server, switch to the Routing and Remote Access console.

14. Select the Remote Access Clients node and, if necessary, press the F5 key to refresh the display.

15. Double-click the client connection from your partner server. A Status dialog box appears.

16. Take a screen shot of the Status dialog box by pressing Ctrl+Prt Scr and then paste the resulting image into the Lab10_worksheet file in the page provided by pressing Ctrl+V.

17. In the Status dialog box, click *Disconnect*. Then click *Close*. The connection disappears from the Routing and remote Access console.

18. Close the Routing and Remote Access console.

19. Close the Network and Sharing Center control panel.

Exercise 10.6	Restoring TCP/IP Settings
Overview	Once you have completed your work with Routing and Remote Access Services, you can return your server back to its original TCP/IP configuration.
Completion time	5 minutes

1. In the *Initial Configuration Tasks* window, click *Configure networking*. The Network Connections window appears.

2. Right-click the *Local Area Connection icon* and, from the context menu, select *Properties*. The Local Area Connection Properties sheet appears.

3. Select Internet Protocol Version 4 (TCP/IPv4) and click *Properties. The Internet Protocol Version 4 (TCP/IPv4) Properties* sheet appears.

4. In the IP address text box, type **10.0.xx.1**, where *xx* is the number your instructor assigned to your server.

5. In the Subnet mask text box, type **255.255.255.0**.

6. In the Default gateway text box, remove the current setting and leave the box blank.

7. Leave the Preferred DNS server text box set to 127.0.0.1.

8. Click *OK* to close the Internet Protocol Version 4 (TCP/IPv4) Properties sheet.

9. Click *OK* to close the Local Area Connection Properties sheet.

10. Close the Network Connections window.

11. Log off of the server.

LAB 11
USING DATA MANAGEMENT SOLUTIONS

This lab contains the following exercises and activities:3

Exercise 11.1   Installing the DFS Role Service

Exercise 11.2   Creating a DFS Namespace

Exercise 11.3   Adding a Folder to a Namespace

Exercise 11.4   Duplicating Folders and Servers

BEFORE YOU BEGIN

The lab environment consists of student servers connected to a local area network, along with a classroom server that functions as the domain controller for a domain called contoso.com. Each student has his or her own server, which functions as a domain controller for a separate forest. Most of the exercises in this manual will require each student to work on his or her own domain controller in a separate Active Directory Domain Services domain.

> *In the classroom lab environment, the instructor has assigned each server a number that the student will use to form the server's IP address, computer name, and domain name, as specified in Lab 1. This will keep each server in its own separate environment and prevent server interaction until it is specifically needed. You must complete Lab 1 before you proceed with the exercises in this lab.*

In addition to the computers, you will also require the software listed in Table 11-1 to complete Lab 11.

Table 11-1
Software required for Lab 11

Software	Location
Lab 11 student worksheet	Lab11_worksheet.rtf (provided by instructor)

Working with Lab Worksheets

Each lab in this manual requires that you answer questions, shoot screen shots, and perform other activities that you will document in a worksheet named for the lab, such as Lab11_worksheet.rtf. Your instructor will provide you with access to the worksheets. It is recommended that you use a USB flash drive to store your worksheets, so you can submit them to your instructor for review. As you perform the exercises in each lab, open the appropriate worksheet file using WordPad, fill in the required information, and save the file to your flash drive.

SCENARIO

Contoso, Ltd. has a number of branch offices with users that do not understand how networks and servers function. You have therefore been assigned the task of evaluating data-sharing and management solutions, such as Distributed File System. By creating a DFS namespace on a server at each of these offices, you plan to consolidate the shares on various user workstations into a single entity, accessible to the entire staff.

After completing this lab, you will be able to:

- Install DFS

- Create a DFS namespace

Estimated lab time: 45 minutes

Exercise 11.1	Installing the DFS Role Service
Overview	Install the role service needed to run the Distributed File System.
Completion time	5 minutes

1. Log on to your server using the **Administrator** account and the password **Pa$$w0rd**. The Initial Configuration Tasks window appears.

2. Click *Start*. Then click *Administrative Tools > Server Manager*. The Server Manager console appears.

3. Expand the Roles node and select the File Services node.

4. Scroll down in the detail pane and click the *Add Role Services* link. The Add Role Services wizard appears, displaying the *Select Role Services* page, as shown in Figure 11-1.

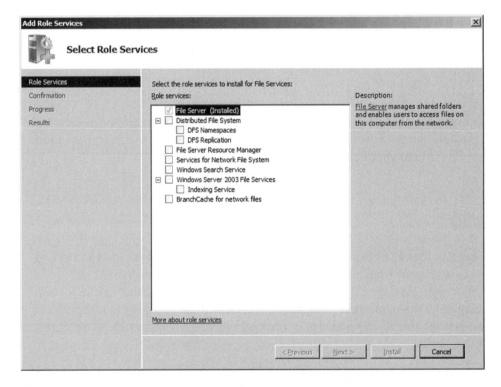

Figure 11-1
The *Select Role Services* page in the Add Role Services Wizard

5. Select the Distributed File System checkbox and click *Next*. The *Create a DFS Namespace* page appears.

6. Select the Create a namespace later using the DFS Management snap-in in Server Manager option and click *Next*. The *Confirm Installation Selections* page appears.

7. Click *Install*. The *Installation Progress* page appears as the wizard installs the role service.

8. Click *Close*. The wizard closes.

9. Leave the Server Manager console open for the next exercise.

Exercise 11.2	Creating a DFS Namespace
Overview	Create a domain-based DFS namespace in which you can store data on various shares all over the network.
Completion time	10 minutes

1. In the Server Manager console, browse to the Roles\File Services\DFS Management node. The DFS Management snap-in appears in the detail pane, as shown in Figure 11-2.

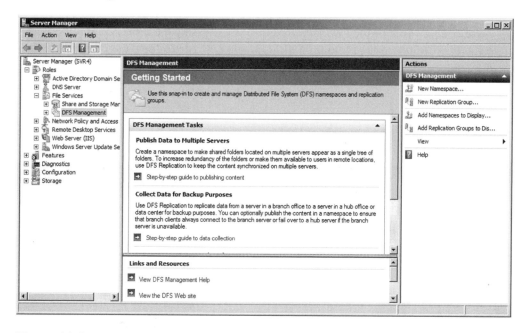

Figure 11-2
The DFS Management snap-in

2. In the actions pane, click *New Namespace*. The New Namespace wizard appears, displaying the *Namespace Server* page.

3. In the Server text box, type **SVR***xx*, where *xx* is the number your instructor assigned to your computer, and click *Next*. The *Namespace Name and Settings* page appears.

4. In the Name text box, type **Contoso***xx* **Docs**, where *xx* is the number your instructor assigned to your computer.

5. Click *Edit Settings*. The Edit Settings dialog box appears.

6. Select the Administrators have full access; other users have read and write permissions option and click *OK*.

7. Click *Next*. The *Namespace Type* page appears.

8. Leave the Domain-based namespace option selected and click *Next*. The *Review Settings and Create Namespace* page appears.

Question 1	What is the path to the DFS namespace you are creating, using the Universal Naming Convention (UNC) format?

9. Click *Create*. The wizard creates the namespace and the *Confirmation* page appears with a success indicator.

10. Take a screen shot of the *Confirmation* page by pressing Ctrl+Prt Scr and then paste the resulting image into the Lab11_worksheet file in the page provided by pressing Ctrl+V.

11. Click *Close*. The wizard closes.

12. Leave the Server Management console open for the next exercise.

Exercise 11.3   Adding a Folder to a Namespace

Overview	Once you have created a standalone DFS namespace, you can add shared folders from any location, making them accessible through the namespace.
Completion time	15 minutes

1. In the Server Manager console, expand the DFS Management node and select the Namespaces node beneath.

2. Select the Contoso04 Docs namespace you created in the detail pane.

3. In the actions pane, select New Folder. The New Folder dialog box appears, as shown in Figure 11-3.

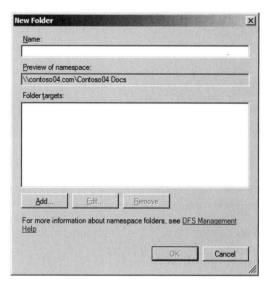

Figure 11-3
The New Folder dialog box

4. In the Name textbox, type **Contracts**.

5. Click *Add*. The Add Folder Target dialog box appears.

6. Click *Browse*. The Browse for Shared Folders dialog box appears.

7. Click *New Shared Folder*. The Create Share dialog box appears.

8. In the Share name text box, type **Contracts**.

9. In the Local path of shared folder text box, type **c:\contracts**.

10. Select the Administrators have full access; other users have read and write permissions option and click *OK*. A Warning message box appears, asking if you want to create the folder.

11. Click *Yes*. The new share appears in the Browse for Shared Folders dialog box.

12. Click *OK*. The share you created appears in the Add Folder Target dialog box.

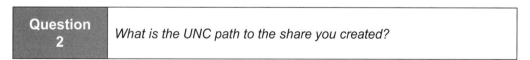

Question 2	What is the UNC path to the share you created?

13. Click *OK*. The share appears in the Folder targets list in the New Folder dialog box.

14. Click *OK*. The folder is added to the namespace.

15. Expand the Namespaces node and select the \\contosoxx.com\Contosoxx Docs namespace. The Contracts folder appears in the detail pane.

16. Take a screen shot of the Server Manager console showing the namespace and the folder by pressing Ctrl+Prt Scr and then paste the resulting image into the Lab11_worksheet file in the page provided by pressing Ctrl+V.

17. Leave the Server Manager console open for the next exercise.

Exercise 11.4	Duplicating Folders and Servers
Overview	DFS enables you to create duplicate folders and duplicate servers for fault-tolerance purposes.
Completion time	15 minutes

1. In the Server Manager console, select the Contracts folder you created in Exercise 11.3. A list of folder targets appears.

2. In the actions pane, click *Add Folder Target*. The New Folder Target dialog box appears.

3. Click *Browse*. The Browse for Shared Folders dialog box appears.

4. Click *New Shared Folder*. The Create Share dialog box appears.

5. In the Share name text box, type **Contracts2**.

6. In the *Local path of shared folder* text box, type **c:\contracts2**.

7. Select the Administrators have full access; other users have read and write permissions option and click *OK*. A Warning message box appears, asking if you want to create the folder.

8. Click *Yes*. The new share appears in the Browse for Shared Folders dialog box.

9. Click *OK*. The share you created appears in the New Folder Target dialog box.

Question 3	*What is the benefit of creating a second target for the same folder?*

10. Click *OK*. A Replication message box appears, offering to create a replication group for the folder targets.

Question 4	*What is the benefit of creating a replication group for the folder targets?*

11. Click *Yes*. An Error message box appears, stating that the folder targets cannot be added as DFS Replication members.

12. Click *Details*. The Error message box expands.

13. Take a screen shot of the expanded Error message box by pressing Ctrl+Prt Scr and then paste the resulting image into the Lab11_worksheet file in the page provided by pressing Ctrl+V.

Question 5	*What must you do to create a folder target that does not generate an error?*

14. Click *OK*. The Error message box closes and the Contracts2 share appears in the Folder Targets list.

15. Select the \\contosoxx.com\Contosoxx Docs namespace.

16. In the actions pane, click *Add Namespace Server*. The Add Namespace Server dialog box appears, as shown in Figure 11-4.

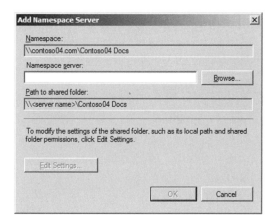

Figure 11-4
The Add Namespace Server dialog box

Question 6	*If creating multiple folder targets provides fault tolerance for the data, what is the benefit of creating another namespace server?*

Question 7	*Why can't you create a second namespace server in your current lab environment?*

17. Click *Cancel*. The Add Namespace Server dialog box closes.

18. Close the Server Manager console.

19. Log off of the server.

LAB 12
BUILDING A PUBLIC KEY INFRASTRUCTURE

This lab contains the following exercises and activities:

Exercise 12.1   Installing Active Directory Certificate Services

Exercise 12.2   Using the Certificates Snap-in

Exercise 12.3   Using Web-based Enrollment

BEFORE YOU BEGIN

The lab environment consists of student servers connected to a local area network, along with a classroom server that functions as the domain controller for a domain called contoso.com. Each student has his or her own server, which functions as a domain controller for a separate forest. Most of the exercises in this manual will require each student to work on his or her own domain controller in a separate Active Directory Domain Services domain.

> NOTE
>
> *In the classroom lab environment, the instructor has assigned each server a number that the student will use to form the server's IP address, computer name, and domain name, as specified in Lab 1. This will keep each server in its own separate environment and prevent server interaction until it is specifically needed. You must complete Lab 1 before you proceed with the exercises in this lab.*

In addition to the computers, you will also require the software listed in Table 12-1 to complete Lab 12.

Table 12-1
Software required for Lab 12

Software	Location
Lab 12 student worksheet	Lab12_worksheet.rtf (provided by instructor)

Working with Lab Worksheets

Each lab in this manual requires that you answer questions, shoot screen shots, and perform other activities that you will document in a worksheet named for the lab, such as Lab12_worksheet.rtf. Your instructor will provide you with access to the worksheets. It is recommended that you use a USB flash drive to store your worksheets, so you can submit them to your instructor for review. As you perform the exercises in each lab, open the appropriate worksheet file using WordPad, fill in the required information, and save the file to your flash drive.

SCENARIO

The IT director wants you to explore the possibility of installing an enterprise certification authority and issuing certificates to users at remote locations for security purposes. Your task is to implement this technology in the lab and examine its capabilities.

After completing this lab, you will be able to:

- Install an enterprise certification authority

- Use the Certificates snap-in

- Use the web enrollment interface

Estimated lab time: 30 minutes

Exercise 12.1	Installing Active Directory Certificate Services
Overview	Install the Active Directory Certificate Services role and configure your server to function as an enterprise root CA.
Completion time	10 minutes

1. Log on to your server using the **Administrator** account and the password **Pa$$w0rd**. The Initial Configuration Tasks window appears.

2. Click *Start*. Then click *Administrative Tools > Server Manager*. The Server Manager console appears.

3.   Select the Roles node and click *Add Roles*. The Add Roles Wizard appears, displaying the *Before You Begin* page.

4.   Click *Next* to continue. The *Select Server Roles* page appears.

5.   Select the Active Directory Certificate Services role and click *Next*. The *Introduction to Active Directory Certificate Services* page appears.

6.   Click *Next* to continue. The *Select Role Services* page appears, as shown in Figure 12-1.

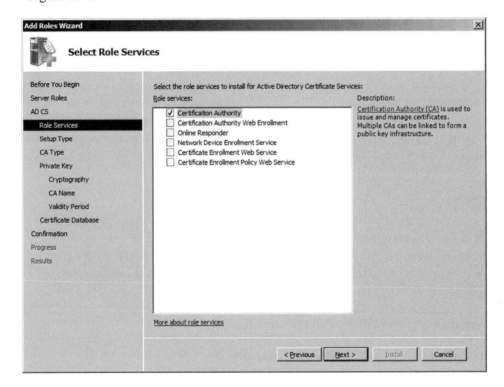

Figure 12-1
The *Select Role Services* page of the Add Roles Wizard

7.   Select the Certification Authority and Certification Authority Web Enrollment check boxes. The Add role services required for Certification Authority Web Enrollment dialog box appears.

8.   Click *Add Required Role Services*. Then click *Next*. The *Specify Setup Type* page appears.

9.   Leave the Enterprise option selected and click *Next*. The *Specify CA Type* page appears.

10.   Leave the Root CA option selected and click *Next*. The *Set Up Private Key* page appears.

11.   Leave the Create a new private key option selected and click *Next*. The *Configure Cryptography for CA* page appears.

12. In the Key character length drop-down list, select 4096 and click *Next*. The *Configure CA Name* page appears.

13. Click *Next* to accept the default CA name. The *Set Validity Period* page appears.

14. Click *Next* to accept the default 5-year validity period. The *Configure Certificate Database* page appears.

15. Click *Next* to accept the default database locations. The *Introduction to Web Server (IIS)* page appears.

16. Click *Next*. The *Select Role Services* page appears.

17. Click *Next* to accept the default role services. The *Confirm Installation Selections* page appears.

18. Click *Install*. The wizard installs the roles and the *Installation Results* page appears.

19. Take a screen shot of the *Installation Results* page by pressing Ctrl+Prt Scr and then paste the resulting image into the Lab12_worksheet file in the page provided by pressing Ctrl+V.

20. Click *Close*. The wizard closes.

21. Click the *Server Manager (SVRxx)* node.

22. In the detail pane, scroll down to the Security Information box and click *Configure IE ESC*. The *Internet Explorer Enhanced Security Configuration* page appears.

23. Under Administrators, select the Off option and click *OK*.

24. Close the Server Manager console.

25. Leave the computer logged on for the next exercise.

Exercise 12.2	Using the Certificates Snap-In
Overview	Test the functionality of your certification authority by requesting a certificate using the Certificates snap-in for Microsoft Management Console.
Completion time	10 minutes

1. Click *Start*. Then click *Run*. The Run dialog box appears.

2. In the Open text box, key **mmc** and click *OK*. A blank Microsoft Management Console window appears.

3. Click *File > Add/Remove Snap-In*. The Add or Remove Snap-ins dialog box appears.

4. In the Available snap-ins list, select Certificates and click *Add*. The Certificates snap-in dialog box appears.

5. Leave the My user account option selected and click *Finish*.

6. Click *OK* to close the Add or Remove Snap-ins dialog box. The Certificates snap-in appears in the MMC console.

7. Expand the Certificates–Current User node, as shown in Figure 12-2.

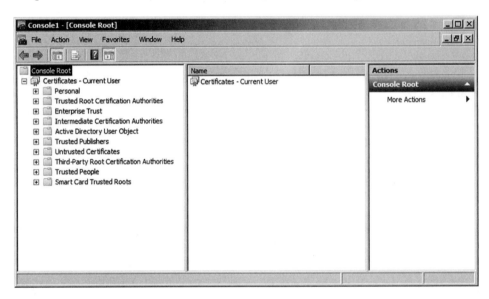

Figure 12-2
The Certificates–Current User console

8. Expand the Trusted Root Certification Authorities folder and select the Certificates folder beneath it.

9. In the list of certificates, locate one called contoso*xx*-SVR*xx*-CA, where *xx* is the number your instructor assigned to your computer, and double-click it. A Certificate dialog box appears.

Question 1	What CA issued this certificate?

10. Take a screen shot of the Certificate dialog box by pressing Ctrl+Prt Scr and then paste the resulting image into the Lab12_worksheet file in the page provided by pressing Ctrl+V.

11. Click *OK* to close the Certificate dialog box.

12. Right-click the *Personal* folder and, from the context menu, select All Tasks > Request New Certificate. The Certificate Enrollment wizard appears, displaying the *Before You Begin* page.

13. Click *Next*. The *Select Certificate Enrollment Policy* page appears.

14. Click *Next* to accept the default policy. The *Request Certificates* page appears.

15. Select the User check box and click *Enroll*. The *Requesting certificates* page appears.

16. Take a screen shot of the *Certificate Installation Results* page by pressing Ctrl+Prt Scr and then paste the resulting image into the Lab12_worksheet file in the page provided by pressing Ctrl+V.

17. Click *Close*.

18. Close the Certificates console

19. Leave the computer logged on for the next exercise.

Exercise 12.3	Using Web-Based Enrollment
Overview	Use your CA's web-based enrollment feature to request a certificate, just as your company's remote users will have to do in the future.
Completion time	10 minutes

1. Click *Start*. Then click *Internet Explorer*. An Internet Explorer window appears, with the Set Up Windows Internet Explorer 8 window on top of it.

2. Click *Ask me later*.

3. In the address box, key **http://svr*xx*/certsrv**, where *xx* is the number your instructor assigned to your server, and press *Enter*. A *Certificate Error: Navigation Blocked* page appears.

4. Click *Continue* to this Web site (not recommended). *The Microsoft Active Directory Certificate Services* page appears, as shown in Figure 12-3.

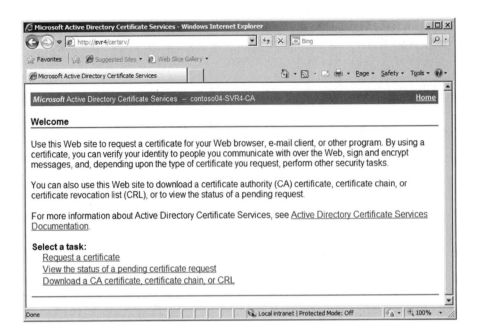

Figure 12-3
The *Microsoft Active Directory Certificate Services* page

5. Click *Request a certificate*. The *Request a Certificate* page appears.

6. Click *Advanced certificate request*. The *Advanced Certificate Request* page appears.

7. Click *Create* and submit a request to this CA. A Web Access Confirmation message box appears, warning that the Web site is attempting to perform a digital certificate operation.

8. Click *Yes*. The *Advanced Certificate Request* page appears.

9. In the Certificate Template drop-down list, select User.

10. Click *Submit*. The *Certificate Issued* page appears.

11. Take a screen shot of the *Certificate Issued* page by pressing Ctrl+Prt Scr and then paste the resulting image into the Lab12_worksheet file in the page provided by pressing Ctrl+V.

12. Click *Install this Certificate*. The *Certificate Installed* page appears.

Question 2	How would this procedure be different if you had created a standalone CA instead of an enterprise CA?

13. Close the Internet Explorer window.

LAB 13
BACKING UP

This lab contains the following exercises and activities:

Exercise 13.1   Installing Windows Server Backup

Exercise 13.2   Creating a Backup Volume

Exercise 13.3   Performing a Single Backup

Exercise 13.4   Performing an Incremental Backup

Exercise 13.5   Recovering Data

BEFORE YOU BEGIN

The lab environment consists of student servers connected to a local area network, along with a classroom server that functions as the domain controller for a domain called contoso.com. Each student has his or her own server, which functions as a domain controller for a separate forest. Most of the exercises in this manual will require each student to work on his or her own domain controller in a separate Active Directory Domain Services domain.

> **NOTE**
>
> *In the classroom lab environment, the instructor has assigned each server a number that the student will use to form the server's IP address, computer name, and domain name, as specified in Lab 1. This will keep each server in its own separate environment and prevent server interaction until it is specifically needed. You must complete Lab 1 before you proceed with the exercises in this lab.*

In addition to the computers, you will also require the software listed in Table 13-1 to complete Lab 13.

Table 13-1
Software required for Lab 13

Software	Location
Lab 13 student worksheet	Lab13_worksheet.rtf (provided by instructor)

Working with Lab Worksheets

Each lab in this manual requires that you answer questions, shoot screen shots, and perform other activities that you will document in a worksheet named for the lab, such as Lab13_worksheet.rtf. Your instructor will provide you with access to the worksheets. It is recommended that you use a USB flash drive to store your worksheets, so you can submit them to your instructor for review. As you perform the exercises in each lab, open the appropriate worksheet file using WordPad, fill in the required information, and save the file to your flash drive.

SCENARIO

Your assignment today in your company's network test lab is to examine the capabilities of the Windows Server Backup tool included in Windows Server 2008 R2.

After completing this lab, you will be able to:

- Install Windows Server Backup

- Create backup jobs

- Restore data from backups

Estimated lab time: 70 minutes

Exercise 13.1	Installing Windows Server Backup
Overview	Install the backup software that is included as a feature with Windows Server 2008 R2.
Completion time	5 minutes

1. Log on to your server using the **Administrator** account and the password **Pa$$w0rd**. The Initial Configuration Tasks window appears.

2. Click *Start*. Then click *Administrative Tools > Server Manager*. The Server Manager console appears.

3. In the scope pane, select the Features node.

4. In the detail pane, click *Add Features*. The Add Features Wizard appears, displaying the *Select Features* page.

5. Expand Windows Server Backup Features, and then select the Windows Server Backup and Command-line Tools checkboxes, as shown in Figure 13-1.

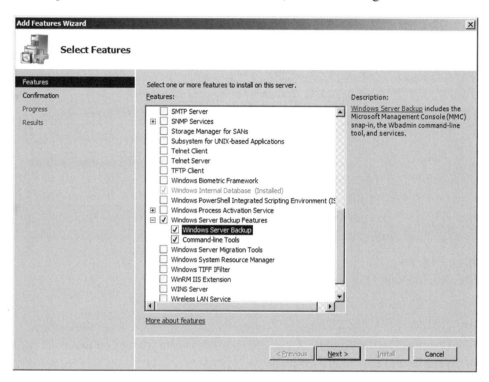

Figure 13-1
The Windows Server Backup Features

6. Click *Next*. The *Confirm Installation Selections* page appears.

7. Click *Install*. The wizard installs the features.

8. Click *Close*. The wizard closes.

9. Close the Server Manager console.

10. Leave the computer logged on for the next exercise.

Exercise 13.2	Creating a Backup Volume
Overview	Create the volume that you will use to back up your Windows Server 2008 computer.
Completion time	10 minutes

1. Click *Start*. Then click *Administrative Tools > Computer Management*. The Computer Management console appears.

2. Select the Disk Management node, as shown in Figure 13-2.

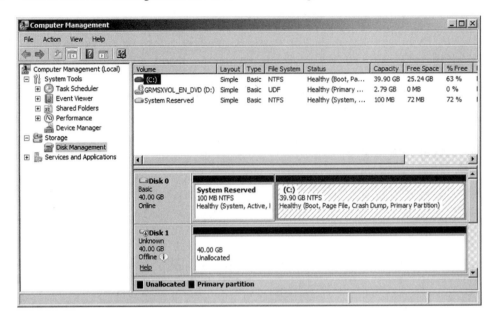

Figure 13-2
The Disk Management snap-in

3. If there are any volumes on Disk 1, right-click each one and, from the context menu, select Delete Volume. A message box appears warning you that deleting the volume will erase any data on it.

4. Click *Yes*. The volume is deleted.

5. When all of the space on Disk 1 is unallocated, right-click the unallocated space and, from the context menu, select New Simple Volume. The New Simple Volume Wizard appears.

6. Click *Next* to bypass the *Welcome* page. The *Specify Volume Size* page appears.

7. Click *Next* to use all of the available space for the volume. The *Assign Drive Letter or Path* page appears.

8. In the Assign the following drive letter drop-down list, select letter Z. Then click *Next*. The *Format Partition* page appears.

9. In the Volume label text box, type **Backup**.

10. Select the Perform a quick format check box and click *Next*. The *Completing the New Simple Volume Wizard* page appears.

11. Click *Finish*. The wizard creates the volume.

12. Take a screen shot of the Computer Management console, showing the volume(s) you just created, by pressing Ctrl+Prt Scr, and then paste the resulting image into the Lab13_worksheet file in the page provided by pressing Ctrl+V.

13. Close the Computer Management console.

14. Leave the computer logged on for the next exercise.

Exercise 13.3	Performing a Single Backup
Overview	Perform a single backup of your computer to the backup volume you created in Exercise 13.2.
Completion time	20 minutes

1. Click *Start*. Then click *Administrative Tools > Windows Server Backup*. The Windows Server Backup console appears, as shown in Figure 13-3.

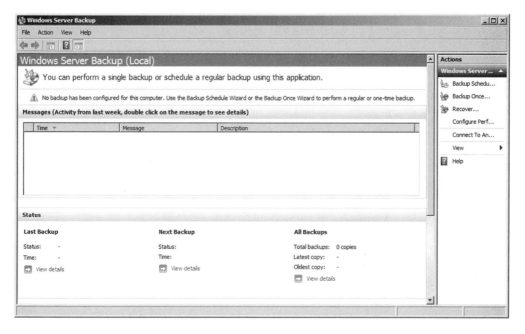

Figure 13-3
The Windows Server Backup console

2. In the actions pane, click *Backup Once*. The Backup Once Wizard appears, displaying the *Backup options* page.

3. Leave the Different options option selected and click *Next*. The *Select backup configuration* page appears.

4. Leave the Full server (recommended) option selected and click *Next*. The *Specify destination type* page appears.

5. Leave the Local drives option selected and click *Next*. The *Select backup destination* page appears.

6.   In the Backup destination drop-down list, select Backup (Z:) and click *Next*. A Windows Server Backup message box appears, warning that the backup destination is included in the list of items to back up. Click *OK* to exclude it. The *Confirmation* page appears.

7.   Click *Backup*. The *Backup progress* page appears and the backup begins.

8.   When the backup is completed, take a screen shot of the *Backup progress* page by pressing Ctrl+Prt Scr and then paste the resulting image into the Lab13_worksheet file in the page provided by pressing Ctrl+V.

9.   Click *Close*. The wizard closes.

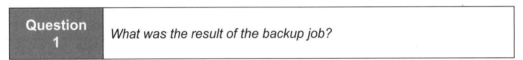

Question 1	*What was the result of the backup job?*

10. Leave the Windows Server Backup console open for the next exercise.

Exercise 13.4   Running an Incremental Backup

Overview	Demonstrate how incremental backups save time and media.
Completion time	20 minutes

1.   In the Windows Server Backup console, in the Status area, under Last Backup, click *View details*. The Details – Last Backup dialog box appears, as shown in Figure 13-4.

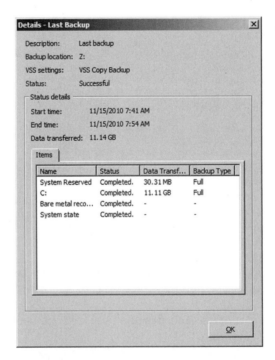

Figure 13-4
The Details – Last Backup dialog box

2.   In your worksheet, fill out Table 13-2, using the information from the Details –
     Last Backup dialog box.

Table 13-2

Drive	Data Transferred	Backup Type
System Reserved		
C:		

3.   Click *OK* to close the Details – Last Backup dialog box.

4.   In the actions pane, click *Configure Performance Settings*. The Optimize Backup
     Performance dialog box appears, as shown in Figure 13-5.

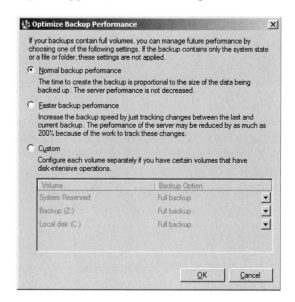

Figure 13-5
The Optimize Backup Performance dialog box

5.   Select the *Faster backup performance* option and click *OK*.

Question 2	How does an incremental job increase the overall speed of the backup process?

6.   Click *Start*. Then click *All Programs > Accessories > Windows Explorer*. A
     Windows Explorer window appears.

7.   Browse to the C:\Windows folder and double-click the WindowsUpdate text
     document file. A Notepad window appears, containing the contents of the file.

8.   Type your name into the top line of the file and click *File > Save As*. The Save As combo box appears.

9.   Save the file to the Favorites\Downloads folder and close the Notepad window.

10.   Click *Start*. Then click *All Programs > Accessories*.

11.   Right-click *Command Prompt* and, from the context menu, select Run as Administrator. A Command Prompt window appears.

12.   On your worksheet, write out a command using the Wbadmin.exe program to execute a backup, using the same parameters you specified graphically in Exercise 13.3.

13.   Key your command in the Command Prompt window and press *Enter*. The backup begins.

14.   When the backup is completed, take a screen shot of the Windows Server Backup console, showing the successful results, by pressing Ctrl+Prt Scr and then paste the resulting image into the Lab13_worksheet file in the page provided by pressing Ctrl+V.

15.   In the Windows Server Backup console, in the Status area, under Last Backup, click *View details*. The Details – Last Backup dialog box appears.

Question 3	*What type of backup job did you just perform from the Command Prompt, full or incremental?*

16.   Repeat steps 2 to 7 from Exercise 13.3 to run another single backup, using the same parameters.

17.   Open the Details – Last Backup dialog box.

18.   In your worksheet, fill out Table 13-3, using the information from the Details – Last Backup dialog box.

Table 13-3

Drive	*Data Transferred*	*Backup Type*
System Reserved		
C:		

19.   Click *OK* to close the Details – Last Backup dialog box.

20.   Leave the Windows Server Backup console open for the next exercise.

Exercise 13.5 Recovering Data

Overview	Recover data from your most recent backup job.
Completion time	15 minutes

1. In the Windows Server Backup console, in the actions pane, click *Recover*. The Recovery Wizard appears, displaying the *Getting started* page, as shown in Figure 13-6.

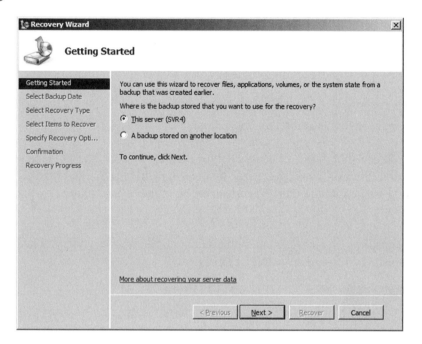

Figure 13-6
The Recovery Wizard

2. Click *Next* to accept the default This server setting. The *Select backup date* page appears.

3. With today's date selected in the calendar, expand the Time drop-down list.

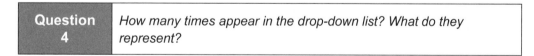

Question 4	*How many times appear in the drop-down list? What do they represent?*

4. Select the most recent time in the drop-down list and click *Next*. The *Select recovery type* page appears.

5. Leave the Files and folders option selected and click *Next*. The *Select items to recover* page appears.

6. In the Available items list, expand the SVRxx and Local disk (C:) folders and select the Users folder. The contents of the Users folder appears.

7. With the contents of the Users folder selected, click *Next*. The *Specify recovery options* page appears.

8. In the Recovery destination box, select the Another location option and click *Browse*. The Browse For Folder dialog box appears.

9. Browse to the C: volume and click *Make New Folder*.

10. Give the new folder the name Recovered Data and click *OK*. The path to the new folder appears in the *Another location* text box.

11. Click *Next*. The *Confirmation* page appears.

12. Click *Recover*. The Recovery progress window appears and the recovery job starts.

13. When the recovery is complete, click *Close*.

14. Take a screen shot of the Windows Server Backup console, showing the successful result of the recovery job, by pressing Ctrl+Prt Scr and then paste the resulting image into the Lab13_worksheet file in the page provided by pressing Ctrl+V.

15. In the console's Messages area, double-click the file recovery job you just performed. A *File recovery* dialog box appears.

Question 5	*How much data was transferred during the recovery job?*

Question 6	*How can you explain the amount of data that was transferred during the recovery job, as compared to the amount of data transferred during the incremental backup job from which you are recovering data, as shown in Table 13-3?*

16. Click *OK* to close the *File recovery* dialog box.

17. Close the Windows Server Backup console.

18. Log off of the computer.

APPENDIX:
LAB SETUP GUIDE

This appendix describes the process by which instructors teaching the course in a standard wired classroom lab should set up and install the servers and workstations students will need to complete the exercises in the lab manual. This setup guide can also be adapted for use with a workstation-based virtual machine environment such as Microsoft Virtual PC. For instructors using MOAC Labs Online, no setup or installation is necessary, as the virtual machines in the online labs are pre-configured and ready for students to use.

The Windows Server 2008 Enterprise Administrator title of the Microsoft Official Academic Course (MOAC) series includes two books: a textbook and a lab manual. The exercises in the lab manual are designed either for a virtual machine environment or for classroom use under the supervision of an instructor or lab aide. In an academic setting, the computer lab may be used by a variety of classes each day, so you must plan your setup procedure accordingly. For example, consider automating the classroom setup procedure and using removable hard disks in the classroom. You can use the automated setup procedure to rapidly configure the classroom environment, and remove the fixed disks after teaching this class each day.

LAB CONFIGURATION

This course should be taught in a lab containing networked computers on which students can develop their skills through hands-on experience with Microsoft Windows Server 2008 R2. The exercises in the lab manual require the computers to be installed and configured in a specific manner. Failure to adhere to the setup instructions in this document can produce unanticipated results when the students perform the exercises.

The lab configuration consists of a number of student servers running Windows Server 2008 R2 Enterprise. Each student server is connected to a classroom network equipped with a router providing access to the Internet. In the absence of an Internet connection, a single classroom server, also running Windows Server 2008 R2 Enterprise, can give the students access to the software products they require.

Each student computer in the classroom will be configured (by the students) as an Active Directory Domain Services (AD DS) domain controller for a forest separate from the rest of the school or organization network. If present, the classroom server also functions as a Active Directory Domain Services domain controller for its own forest.

133

The setup procedure for the student servers consists only of a standard operating installation procedure. The students will perform all of the additional server configuration tasks in the course of the labs.

The instructor must assign each student server a number, represented throughout the lab manual by the variable *xx*. The students will use this number to form the computer names (SVR*xx*), domain names (contoso*xx*.com), and IP addresses (10.0.*xx*.1) they will need to configure their servers.

> **NOTE**
>
> *For the purposes of this lab, all server and workstation passwords, for user acounts and other purposes, will be set to **Pa$$w0rd**. This is obviously not a secure practice in a real-world situation, and instructors should remind students of this at the outset.*

Some of the lab exercises have dependencies on previous exercises, as noted in the lab manual and the instructor notes for each exercise. Students should perform the lab exercises in order, and may have to complete any exercises they missed due to absence before proceeding to the next lab.

Student Server Requirements

The computers running Windows Server 2008 R2 in the classroom require the following hardware and software:

Hardware Requirements

- Minimum: 1.4 GHz x64 processor

- Minimum: 512 MB RAM (3 GB recommended)

- Minimum: 40 GB hard drive

- DVD drive

- 40 GB second hard drive (internal or external) for backup

- Network interface adapter

- Minimum: Super VGA (800x600) display

- Keyboard

- Mouse

> **NOTE**
>
> *By the end of the course, students will have installed a large number of roles on their lab servers, requiring a significant amount of system resources. If the classroom computers do not have sufficient memory to support all of these roles simultaneously, students may have to remove some roles at various points in the course.*

Software Requirements

All of the software listed below is required on the server:

- Microsoft Windows Server 2008 R2 Enterprise evaluation edition—available as a free download from Microsoft's Web site at http://www.microsoft.com/windowsserver2008/en/us/trial-software.aspx

- Microsoft SQL Server 2005 Express SP3—available as a free download from Microsoft's Web site at http://www.microsoft.com/downloads/en/details.aspx?FamilyID=3181842a-4090-4431-acdd-9a1c832e65a6

- Microsoft Active Directory Migration Tool 3.2—available as a free download from Microsoft's Web site at http://www.microsoft.com/downloads/details.aspx?familyid=20C0DB45-DB16-4D10-99F2-539B7277CCDB&displaylang=en

With the exception of the Windows Server 2008 R2 operating system itself, the software products listed here do not have to be installed on the server prior to the beginning of the course. The students will download them from the Internet during the labs and install them themselves at various points in the course.

If an Internet connection is not available in the classroom, the instructor will have to download these products and make them available to the students on a classroom server or by some other distribution medium.

Network Requirements

The lab manual assumes that the classroom network is using the IPv4 network address 10.0.0.0/24, with the address 10.0.0.1 assigned to the router providing access to the Internet. However, during most of the labs, the students will configure their servers to use IP addresses on a different network: 10.0.xx.0/24. The purpose of this is to isolate each server on its own separate subnet.

Several of the labs require access to the Internet, and those labs begin with an exercise in which the students reconfigure their servers with an address on the 10.0.0.0/24 network. These same labs end with an exercise instructing the students to restore their original IP addresses.

STUDENT SERVER SETUP INSTRUCTIONS

Installing the Student Servers

Overview	Using the following procedure, install Windows Server 2008 R2 on each of your student servers. This procedure assumes that you are performing a clean installation of the Windows Server 2008 R2 Enterprise evaluation edition, and that, if you have downloaded an image file, you have already burned it to a DVD-ROM disk.
Completion time	20 minutes

> **NOTE**
>
> *By performing the following setup instructions, your computer's hard disks will be repartitioned and reformatted. You will lose all existing data on these systems.*

1. Turn the computer on and insert the Windows Server 2008 R2 installation DVD into the drive.

2. Press any key, if necessary, to boot from the DVD-ROM disk. The Setup program loads, and the Install Windows window appears.

3. Modify the *Language to install, Time and currency format*, and *Keyboard or input method* settings, if necessary, and click *Next*.

4. Click *Install Now*. The *Select the operating system you want to install* page appears.

5. Select Windows Server 2008 R2 Enterprise (Full Installation) and click *Next*. The *Please read the license terms* page appears.

6. Select the I accept the license terms check box and click *Next*. The *Which type of installation do you want?* page appears.

7. Click *Custom (advanced)*. The *Where do you want to install Windows?* page appears.

8. Select Disk 0 Unallocated Space and click *Next*. The *Installing Windows* page appears, indicating the progress of the Setup program as it installs the operating system. After the installation completes and the computer restarts, a message appears stating that *The user's password must be changed before logging on the first time*.

9. Click *OK*. A Windows logon screen appears.

10. In the New password and Confirm Password text boxes, type **Pa$$w0rd** and click the right-arrow button. A message appears stating that *Your password has been changed.*

11. Click *OK*. The logon process completes and the Initial Configuration Tasks window appears.

Once the installation process is finished, the instructor has no other setup tasks to complete on the student servers. The students will perform all of the remaining configuration procedures themselves during the labs, including time zone settings, TCP/IP configuration, and installation of Active Directory Domain Services.